GLOBAL TRENDS:
Prospects for Development and Peace

GLOBAL TRENDS:
Prospects for Development and Peace

Volume 1

Edited by
Development and Peace Foundation (sef:)
Institut für Entwicklung und Frieden (INEF)

In memory of Franz Nuscheler,
scholar, academic teacher
and creative mover,
long-time supporter of sef:
and founding director of INEF

Cornelia Ulbert
Marcus Kaplan (eds.)

GLOBAL TRENDS: Prospects for Development and Peace

Multilateral Cooperation for People and Planet

Verlag Barbara Budrich
Opladen • Berlin • Toronto 2026

This open access publication was published with the support of the Open Book Collective and our Library Supporters.

Carbon compensated production

This book is available as a free download from www.budrich.eu (https://doi.org/10.3224/84743196).

ISBN 978-3-8474-3196-1 (Paperback)
eISBN 978-3-8474-3334-7 (PDF)
DOI 10.3224/84743196

Verlag Barbara Budrich GmbH
Stauffenbergstr. 7. D-51379 Leverkusen Opladen, Germany
86 Delma Drive. Toronto, ON M8W 4P6 Canada

A CIP catalogue record for this book is available from Die Deutsche Nationalbibliothek (The German National Library) (https://portal.dnb.de)

Cover design by Chris Langohr Design, March, Germany – chrislangohr-design.de
Typesetting by Michaela Moreels, Saarbrücken, Germany
Editing by Máiréad Collins, Belfast, UK
Printed in Europe on FSC®-certified paper by Elanders Waiblingen GmbH, Waiblingen, Germany

TABLE OF CONTENTS

PREFACE

With this volume in the new series “Global Trends: Perspectives for Development and Peace,” the Institute for Development and Peace (INEF) at the University of Duisburg-Essen and the Development and Peace Foundation (sef:) in Bonn are continuing their long-standing tradition of scientifically analyzing and illuminating current and future challenges in a globalized world against the backdrop of longer-term trends. At the same time, the aim is to identify options for action to address upcoming global problems. The contributions present facts and scientific findings in a way that is particularly useful for political decision-makers and their advisors, enabling them to make informed decisions. However, we also want to use the new booklet series to provide orientation to a broader interested public in academia, civil society, and the media.

The new series thus follows on from the book series “Global Trends”, which INEF and sef: published from 1991 to 2015. Using the format of a booklet series, in which we aim to highlight trends in the areas of “Global Governance for Sustainable Development,” “Peace and Security,” “Global Economy,” and “Environment and Natural Resources”, we strive to present a broad spectrum of international challenges in a comprehensive overview and create cross-links between the individual policy sectors. The first issue of the new series is dedicated to the topic of “Multilateral Cooperation for People and Planet.” With global power structures and concepts of order changing and autocratic tendencies on the rise, many observers are questioning whether multilateral cooperation is still possible at all. The contributions in this volume show that we still need global and multilateral cooperation, and that it is in fact still possible.

We would like to thank all our colleagues who supported us as editors in the production of this volume. Several colleagues from INEF contributed as authors, while others provided helpful feedback during the process. In addition, the team of INEF research assistants, Marie Dera, Pauline Hörschelmann, and Jonathan Jesse, were an indispensable help in creating the illustrations and in the final editing. Finally, we would like to express our sincere thanks to Verlag Barbara Budrich, and particularly Franziska Deller, for their consistently excellent and reliable cooperation.

Cornelia Ulbert (INEF) and Marcus Kaplan (sef:)

LIST OF FIGURES AND TABLES

LIST OF FIGURES

INTRODUCTION

GLOBAL GOVERNANCE FOR SUSTAINABLE DEVELOPMENT

PEACE AND SECURITY

GLOBAL ECONOMY

ENVIRONMENT AND NATURAL RESOURCES

LIST OF TABLES

INTRODUCTION

GLOBAL GOVERNANCE FOR SUSTAINABLE DEVELOPMENT

ENVIRONMENT AND NATURAL RESOURCES

LIST OF ABBREVIATIONS

AI	Artificial Intelligence
ANCIP	African Non-Military Conflict Intervention Practices
APSA	African Peace and Security Architecture
ASEAN	Association of Southeast Asian Nations
AU	African Union
BAFA	Bundesamt für Wirtschaft und Ausfuhrkontrolle (German Federal Office for Economic Affairs and Export Control)
CSDDD	Corporate Sustainability Due Diligence Directive (European Union directive)
CSRD	Corporate Sustainability Reporting Directive (European Union directive)
DPGA	Digital Public Goods Alliance
DRC	Democratic Republic of the Congo
E. P. A.	Environmental Protection Agency (U. S. government agency)
ECOWAS	Economic Community of West African States
ESG	Environmental, Social, and Governance-related
ESRS	European Sustainability Reporting Standards
EU	European Union
EUDR	European Union Deforestation Regulation
G20	Group of 20
GDPR	General Data Protection Regulation (European Union regulation)
GPAI	General Purpose AI Models
GVCs	Global Value Chains
HIPPO Report	Report of the High-Level Independent Panel on Peace Operations
ICANN	Internet Corporation for Assigned Names and Numbers

ICTs	Information and Communication Technologies
IFC	International Finance Corporation
IGO	International Governmental Organization
ILO	International Labour Organization
INGO	International Nongovernmental Organization
ITU	International Telecommunication Union
LDCs	Least Developed Countries
LksG	Lieferkettensorgfaltspflichtengesetz (German Supply Chain Due Diligence Act)
LLDCs	Landlocked Developing Countries
MENA	Middle East and North Africa
MNE	Multinational Enterprise
MNJTF-AI	Multinational Joint Task Force Accra Initiative
MRC	Mekong River Commission
NBI	Nile Basin Initiative
NGOs	Nongovernmental Organizations
OECD	Organization for Economic Co-operation and Development
OSCE	Organization for Security and Co-operation in Europe
P5	Permanent Five (permanent members of the United Nations Security Council)
PRIF	Peace Research Institute Frankfurt
RBOs	River Basin Organizations
RECs	Regional Economic Communities
SDGs	Sustainable Development Goals
SIDS	Small Island Developing States
SIPRI	Stockholm International Peace Research Institute
SPMs	Special Political Missions
TNCs	Transnational Corporations
UN	United Nations
UNCBD	United Nations Convention on Biological Diversity
UNCCD	United Nations Convention to Combat Desertification

UNCTC	United Nations Commission on Transnational Corporations
UNDP	United Nations Development Programme
UNECE	United Nations Economic Commission for Europe
UNESCO	United Nations Educational, Scientific and Cultural Organization
UNFCCC	United Nations Framework Convention on Climate Change
UNGPs	United Nations Guiding Principles on Business and Human Rights
UNHCR	United Nations High Commissioner on Human Rights
UNICEF	United Nations Children's Fund
UNWC	Convention on the Law of the Non-navigational Uses of International Watercourses, "UN Watercourses Convention"
WASH	Water, Sanitation and Hygiene

INTRODUCTION

COMMON GROUND AMID DIFFERENCE: MULTILATERAL COOPERATION FOR PEOPLE AND PLANET

Cornelia Ulbert

Abstract: There is growing consensus that the liberal international order as we have known it is dwindling. Since it never really lived up to its expectations, proponents and critics alike do not think it should be reinvigorated. The new world order that is taking shape is a "multiplex" one, characterized by a plurality of actors and a great political, ideological, and cultural diversity. In contrast to competing models of world order, multiplexity does not see traditional forms of power as the main driver, but rather the interaction capacity of actors that can, for example, be derived from the capacity to reach agreements. However, the contestation of the liberal values still enshrined in the multilateral system of cooperation seems to weaken this capacity. This introductory chapter argues that multilateralism is not only a means to an end but has the social purpose of enabling interaction based on core values – like a spirit of collectivity, inclusivity over exclusivity and negotiated governance – whose observance determines its quality. In the face of growing illiberalism, however, these values are challenged. Nevertheless, global problems that transcend national borders still require multilateral cooperation. As the introduction and the following chapters show, this will be possible but will probably take different forms and should allow political contestation in a pragmatic and pluralistic way.

1. INTRODUCTION

In her State of the Union Address of 10 September 2025 the President of the European Commission, Ursula von der Leyen, emphatically stressed that "Europe is in a fight." She argued that "[b]attlelines for a new world order based on power are being drawn right now." Therefore, this "must be Europe's Independence Moment" (European Commission 2025: 1). The mood which is reflected in this speech is based on impressions caused by a series of crises starting in the 2010s with surging numbers of refugees worldwide due to a rising number of intra-state conflicts,[1] the failure of liberal peacebuilding missions, the COVID-19 pandemic, the Russian invasion of Ukraine, the Hamas attack on Israel and the subsequent war in Gaza, and ultimately, the re-election of Donald Trump as President of the United States, imposing tariffs erratically on almost every country, questioning old alliances and, above all, the international commitment not only of the United States, but the multilateral system on the whole. In contrast, other, longer-term problems, like fighting poverty and inequality, or environment-related challenges with massive economic and social impacts like climate change, biodiversity loss, the looming water crisis or the prevalent plastic waste seem to have been pushed into the background.

At first glance, the prospects for multilateral cooperation seem quite dismal. The more so, since we can see an increase in autocratic regimes and the democratic backsliding[2] of established democracies like the United States. It is no coincidence that the decline of the liberal international order has been discussed for about a decade now, after the first Trump administration came into office in 2017. The rise of populist movements, also in democratic countries, is accompanied not only by questioning the legitimacy of domestic institutions but also by re-claiming national sovereignty, which is usually equated with weakening international institutions or even the withdrawal from them. There is much talk of "independence" and making your own country "great again".

On what kind of "power", as indicated by Ursula von der Leyen, will "order" be based in a globalized interdependent world of the 21st century? What kind of "order" will emerge or has already been emerging while the liberal international order has been dwindling? And will the new order impair or even foreclose multilateral cooperation? Or will it contribute to reinvigorating multilateral cooperation? This introduction and the following chapters argue that we are still in need of global and multilateral cooperation – and it is and will still be possible. Very likely, it will have to take different forms, though, and allow political contestation in a pragmatic and pluralistic way.

---

1 Between 2014 and 2024 the number of forcibly displaces persons doubled from about 60 million in 2014 to more than 123 million in 2024 with 73% hosted in low- and middle-income countries (UNHCR 2025: 1).

2 "By backsliding we mean the incremental erosion of democratic institutions, rules and norms that results from the actions of duly elected governments, typically driven by an autocratic leader" (Haggard/Kaufman 2021: 1).

2. AFTER LIBERAL HEGEMONY: WHAT'S NEXT?

When the United Kingdom decided to leave the European Union (EU) and Donald Trump was elected to his first presidency in 2016, a lively debate about the state of the liberal international order started. Some observers called it "rigged" and demanded to "fix it now or watch it wither" (Colgan/Keohane 2017). Outspoken critics of the liberal international order even proclaimed that the era "after liberal hegemony" (Acharya 2017) had dawned. Meanwhile, many experts believe that what was once called "liberal international order" does not exist anymore. To understand why this is the case and what kind of international order will be and already has been emerging, we have to take a closer look at the reasons for its decay.

2.1 THE DEMISE OF THE LIBERAL INTERNATIONAL ORDER

The liberal international order that was created after World War II, under the auspices of the "benign hegemon" of the United States, resulted in a system of rules-based multilateralism that originally focussed on promoting free trade as its main objective. However, the kind of economic order that was envisaged was made for the Western world and accompanied by a weak human rights regime of the United Nations (UN) and a Security Council paralyzed by decision-making procedures that allowed the permanent five members China, France, the (then) Soviet Union, the United Kingdom and the United States to block any decision with their veto. Only with the end of the Cold War were multilateral institutions, especially of the UN system, entrusted with strengthening human rights and promoting democracy and the rule of law on a global level (Börzel/Zürn 2021: 282–283).

Hence, the liberal international order that was established after the Cold War is characterized by distinct ideational and institutional properties (cf. Goddard et al. 2024: 3): On an ideational level, core liberal values suggest promoting the rights of the individual and enhancing its welfare. Therefore, the purpose of liberal institutions is to curb the state's power vis-à-vis its citizens. On an institutional level, liberal values lead to decision rules that foster inclusive, equal and fair participation as well as equality before the law.

Equipped with such a social purpose and aspiring to realize the decision rules according to liberal values, the system of global governance that was created during the 1990s has contributed to increasing not only the authority of multilateral institutions epitomized by a series of landmark conferences,[3] in which new conventions and norms with varying degrees of commitment were adopted.[4] It also led to an increase in regional intergovernmental organizations and broadened the landscape of actors engaged in global policy processes, including a multitude of stakeholders like Nongovernmental Organizations (NGOs), business and philanthropic foundations. This has also been accompanied by a growing number of international non-state and multistakeholder organizations [see Figure 1] and has gone hand in hand with further institutionalizing norms and rules that help to organize cooperation and provide public goods. Moreover, using the knowledge of scientific experts for policy advice has become increasingly institutionalized, with the Intergovernmental Panel on Climate Change as one of the more prominent examples. At the same time, the 1990s saw the advent of "liberal peacebuilding" associated with not only ending violent (especially intra-state) conflicts but also democratizing post-conflict states and liberalizing their economies as part of a liberal development process.

3 For instance, the UN Conference on Environment and Development in Rio de Janeiro in 1992, The World Conference on Human Rights in Vienna in 1993, the International Conference on Population and Development in Cairo in 1994, the Fourth World Conference on Women in Beijing in China in 1995 or the Millennium Summit in New York in 2000.

4 For instance, as a result of the Rio conference the United Nations Framework Convention on Climate Change (UNFCCC), the Convention on Biological Diversity (UNCBD) or the Convention to Combat Desertification (UNCCD). Other examples are the Beijing Declaration and Platform of Action for the empowerment of women or the adoption of the Millennium Development Goals at the Millennium Summit.

FIGURE 1: Institutional forms of international cooperation have increased due to non-state engagement

Number of international governmental (IGO) and international non-governmental organizations (INGO) (1992–2022)

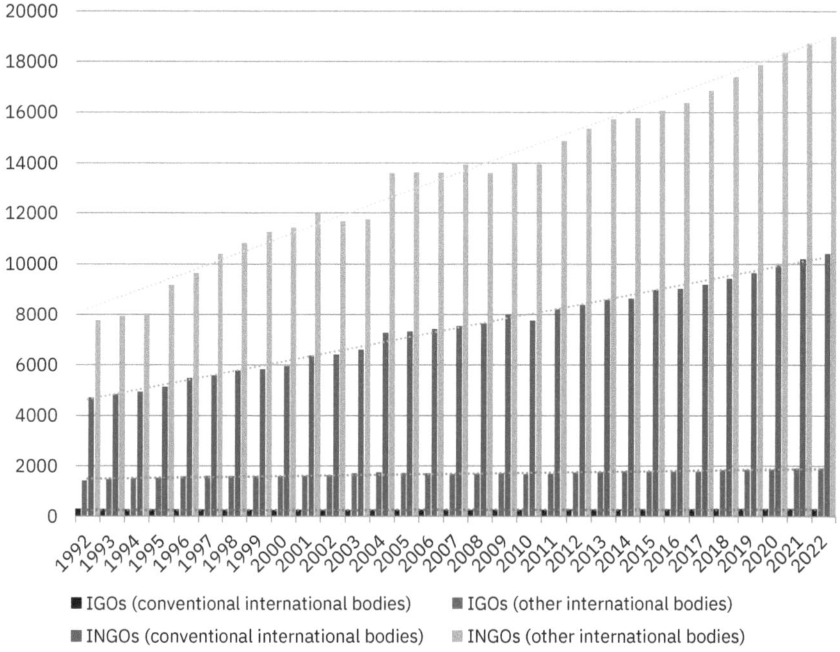

Legend:
Conventional international bodies comprise federations of international organizations, universal membership organizations, intercontinental membership organizations, regionally defined membership organizations.
Other international bodies comprise organizations emanating from places, persons or other bodies, organizations having a special form, including foundations, funds, internationally oriented national organizations.

Source: Union of International Associations 2022: 44–45.

Compared to what the liberal international order promised to achieve, even sympathetic observers must admit that it never lived up to its aspirations and exhibited a good deal of hypocrisy on the part of Western countries (Finnemore 2009: 61). There are several reasons that have contributed to this blunt diagnosis:

- The spread of (nominal) democracies (such as in Eastern Europe) in the 1990s and the increase in economic exchange in the wake of globalization have led to gains in prosperity. However, these are unevenly distributed, leading to increased economic and social inequalities within and between societies worldwide, even in established democracies (Flaherty/Rogowski 2021).

- China, as the most prominent example of a developing country that could reap economic benefits from the liberalization of the global economy and its globalization, has become the main economic competitor of the United States. In turn, the domestic consensus within the United States to support open markets and the institutions associated with it has declined considerably (Weiss/Wallace 2021), as reflected in the protectionist policies of the first and even more the second Trump administration.
- In particular, the "war on terror" made it very clear to other countries that liberal democratic states operate according to double standards, for instance by demanding global compliance with human rights and rule-of-law standards but not consistently adhering to them themselves (see e. g. Birdsall 2016).
- The hope that externally initiated "state-building" would lead to sustainable stability in post-conflict societies *and* to their "modernization" has lately proven illusory, especially in many interventions initiated by Western states. This misjudgement became particularly clear with the hasty withdrawal of Western troops from Afghanistan in August 2021, followed, amongst others, by the termination of the UN-led mission in Mali in December 2023 as ultimately demanded by the military government of Mali.
- Finally, the actions and behaviour of Western countries during the years of the COVID-19 pandemic, characterized by national egoism, have led to a significant decline in their reputation in the countries of the Global South. Consequently, for instance by emphasizing questions of loss and damage due to climate change, the latter are now addressing issues of justice and greater redistribution more forcefully (Lorca 2023).

These developments have led to a loss of legitimacy and growing mistrust of "the West." In contrast, China has been able to gain recognition for its development model in countries of the Global South through increasingly active, primarily bilateral cooperation (see e. g. Hartmann/Noesselt 2020). This also explains why Russia's invasion of Ukraine was not unanimously condemned by an overwhelming majority of countries in the Global South, especially in Africa (Brosig/Verma 2024). The Russian narrative of a West that wanted to annex Ukraine and against whose aggression Russia must now defend itself falls on fertile ground worldwide (Appel 2024). Russia's propagated view of Western liberal democratic societies as "corrupt," "soft," and "decadent" (Riabov/Riabova 2014) resonates also in other countries. In addition, Russia is politically and economically important to many countries in the Global South as a military and security partner (Jacobsen/Larsen 2023) and as exporter of oil, gas, grain and fertilizer.

The list of setbacks of the liberal international order and the open contestation of it, even by its former proponents, does not indicate that the post-Cold War liberal international order will be reinvigorated. Even those in favour of liberal values do not think it should (Goddard et al. 2025: 2). And critics put it quite bluntly that the end of Western dominance will be “a good thing for the world as a whole”, since “the major benefits of the present order have gone disproportionately to the West at the expense of the Rest, thanks to predatory colonization, violence, racism, and injustice” (Acharya 2025: 50). In view of such little support of the current liberal international order how could an emerging or future international order look like?

2.2 COMPETING HIERARCHICAL MODELS OF INTERNATIONAL ORDER

Traditionally, the idea of a stable international order is related to the notion that the international system is hierarchically structured. In other words, a state or groups of states are in command of a considerably greater share of power that enable them to take over a leading position. All current concepts of international order acknowledge that international relations are characterized by different forms of interdependence, i.e. mutual dependence, especially as far as trade and security is concerned [see Table 1]. The liberal international system created after World War II is a distinct type of a hierarchical system led by the United States as benign hegemon. In terms of ideology, security and military might the international order that developed after World War II and lasted until the end of the Cold War is also described as bipolar with two superpowers (Soviet Union and United States) that represented two different political and economic systems. Since the 1990s, the liberal international system dominated by the United States as “indispensable nation” is called a *liberal hegemony*.

TABLE 1: Interaction capacity as main driver leads to a more variable geometry of global governance
Three hierarchical models of international order

	Liberal Hegemony	Multipolarity	Multiplexity
Main driver	Preponderant material power of a single nation (United States)	Approximate equal distribution of material capacity among great powers	Interaction capacity involving state and non-state actors
Leadership	All-embracing: The United States as "indispensable nation" and benign hegemon	Dominated by the great powers	"G-plus" structure
Interdependence	Forged mainly through trade and security links among liberal nations (North-North)	Exclusionary regional blocs in trade and security	Multi-issue besides trade and security (e. g. climate change, pandemics), including North-South and South-South
Global Governance	Centred on big multilaterals of the UN system	Great power competition reduces meaningful cooperation	Variable geometry including layers below the global, starting with the regional

Note: A G-plus structure refers to a world structured by multiple elements exercised by different actors at multiple levels.

Source: Acharya/Estevadeordal/Goodman 2023: 2345 (slightly adapted version).

Many observers look upon the international system of today as one of *multipolarity,* since it is not dominated by only one but several great powers, with their (different kinds of) material capacity approximately equally distributed. In contrast to the liberal hegemony, which furthered multilateral cooperation, especially within the UN system, multipolarity with its great power competition is looked upon as impeding meaningful results of multilateral cooperation, also because of focussing on exclusionary regional blocs (Acharya/Estevadeordal/Goodman 2023: 2359–2360)

An alternative concept of international order is based on the idea of *multiplexity* analogous to a multiplex cinema where a selection of different films is on offer (Acharya 2017: 277). A multiplex order also starts from the assumption that no single global hegemon dominates, although power imbalances and hierarchies still exist. However, instead of looking at the (material) power of the leading states, the interaction capacity of state and non-state actors is seen as the main driver of establishing order. Interaction capacity "is a way of looking at international systems/societies in terms of their carrying capacity for information, goods and people, and the speed, range and cost with which these things can be done" (Buzan 2023: 19). There is a material aspect of interaction capacity that influences the limits and characteristics of every type of exchange from trade to war or even cultural relations. Interaction, however, is also facilitated by primary and secondary institutions: "International law and diplomacy work this way as primary institutions, and secondary institutions such as banking systems and forum organizations like the UN respectively facilitate financial transactions and diplomatic interaction" (Buzan 2023: 19).

In contrast to the other two models of international order, multiplexity acknowledges the diversity of actors that is reflected in the growing number of internationally active non-state organizations [see Figure 1]. Multiplexity also looks at the multitude of interdependent sectoral fields of action that lead to a complex, cross-level architecture of global governance, and great cultural, ideological, and political diversity. An essential feature of multiplexity is its "multiscalarity", i. e. problems exist and interact at multiple scales that transcend clear-cut geographical realms. This entails also that actors do not act on one distinct level only, but across issue areas and levels that are not neatly separated anymore. As a result, the notion of multiplexity describes an international order with a greater variety of interdependent relationships (Acharya/Estevadeordal/Goodman 2023: 2341, 2344).

To establish the amount of interaction capacity one state commands, Acharya et al. use "the ability to negotiate and formalize cooperation through international agreements, including treaty-making" (Acharya/Estevadeordal/Goodman 2023: 2343). The dataset they have constructed does not only encompass the issue areas of economic cooperation or peace and security, but also agreements on natural resources and the environment, human and social development, governance and institutions and what the authors call "connectivity" (cooperation in border management, communication and logistics networks, transportation infrastructure and international migration) (Acharya/Estevadeordal/Goodman

2023: 2346–2347). Like the increase in international institutions, also the overall number of treaties signed within a 15-year period increased steadily with a peak period after the end of the Cold War between 1991 and 2005 [see Figure 2].

FIGURE 2: The contestation of the liberal international order seems to affect the capacity to reach agreements

Treaties signed between 1945 and 2017 by treaty functions

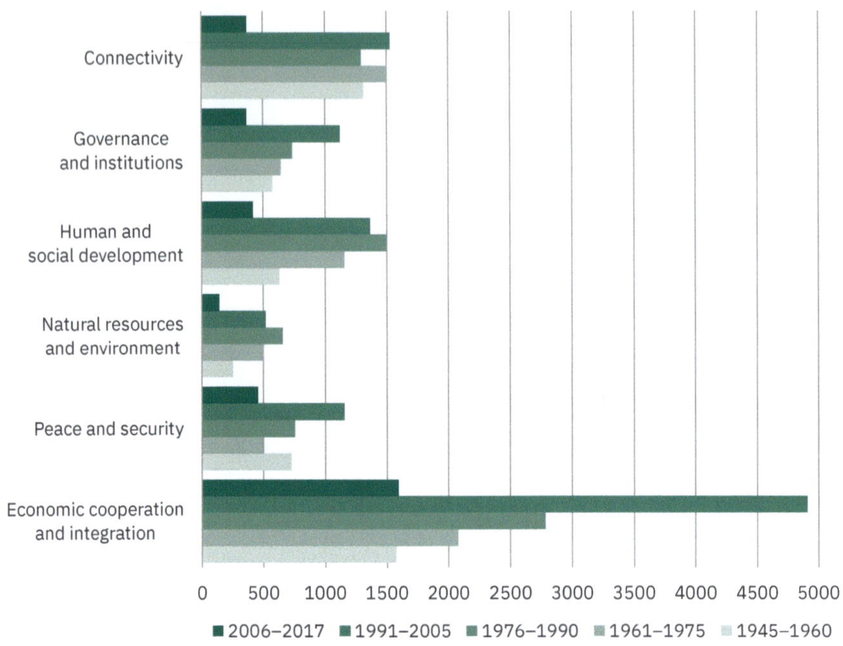

Source: Own depiction based on data of Acharya/Estevadeordal/Goodman 2023: 2351.

The constantly high numbers of treaties relating to economic cooperation and integration reflect the focus of the liberal international order on economic issues. However, starting with the wave of decolonization that manifested itself especially in the 1960s, issues of human and social development also gained prominence. Remarkably, treaty-making on natural resources and environment lags visibly behind all other areas. Many of the problems associated with this issue area belong to the category of "long problems" since their "causes and effects span more than one human generation" (Hale 2024: 3). What is also striking, is the decline of treaty-making after 2006. Although the last period does not cover 15 years like the periods before and although it takes some time between signing and registering a treaty, the numbers seem to reflect the growing contestation of the existing order and its institutions. So, what does this mean for the future of multilateral cooperation?

3. MULTILATERAL COOPERATION IN A MULTIPLEX WORLD

Multilateral cooperation is inextricably linked to the institution of "multilateralism". For years, the overwhelming assessment in politics and academia has been that multilateralism is in crisis. Considering the unresolved problems reflected in the low rate of progress in achieving the UN Sustainable Development Goals (SDGs) in a joint effort, the UN-based multilateralism indeed cannot be called "effective". Especially SDG 2 (Zero Hunger), SDG 11 (Sustainable Cities and Communities), SDG 14 (Life Below Water), SDG 15 (Life on Land) and SDG 16 (Peace, Justice and Strong Institutions) will definitely not be met until 2030 (Sachs et al. 2025: 11). The claim that multilateralism has to be effective is based on a functional view of multilateralism: as long as it delivers results, it "works".

Multilateralism "can be defined as the practice of co-ordinating national policies in groups of three or more states, through ad hoc arrangements or by means of institutions" (Keohane 1990: 731). As John Ruggie pointed out succinctly, this nominal definition does not cover the *qualitative* dimension of multilateralism that distinguishes it from bilateral or other forms of cooperation (Ruggie 1992: 566). For him, "multilateralism refers to coordinating relations among three or more states *in accordance with certain principles*" (Ruggie 1992: 568; emphasis added). In addition, besides providing a formal framework for cooperation, there is also a functional aspect, since "[b]y creating an indivisible collective of equal member states that cooperate across issues based on long-term reciprocity and non-discrimination, multilateralism is assumed to promote stability and predictability in international relations" (Flonk/Debre 2025: 1466). There are strong indications that we can describe the current order as multiplex and that the main driver of this order is the interaction capacity of state and non-state actors in the sense that they are able, among other things, to negotiate and formalize cooperation through inter- or transnational agreements. Then, the question arises, how we can sustain the interaction capacity of the actors involved in global policymaking.

3.1 SUSTAINING INTERACTION CAPACITY: THE VALUE AND QUALITY OF MULTILATERALISM

Traditionally, multilateralism has been looked upon as a means to an end: On the one hand, even less powerful actors were able to raise their voices, and more powerful actors could legitimize how they asserted their interests. On the other hand, the transnational and global nature of many problems simply made it necessary to seek coordinated solutions. Vincent Pouliot, however, also points out, that "governance is not simply about getting things done – it is also, and in fact primarily, about *how* things get done" (Pouliot 2011: 20, emphasis in original). For him, multilateralism as practice promotes certain values, and thus, becomes an end in itself. Since practices structure social interactions, people also develop social relations over time. This helps them to generate common frameworks to assess problems and solutions and define common interests. In many cases this leads actors to (re)define their preferences and interests in the process of interaction (Pouliot 2011: 21–22). It is precisely this relational aspect that makes multilateralism a valuable social practice. To avoid misunderstandings: Actors still do follow their interests. However, their interests are not predetermined.

In contrast to other forms of international cooperation like bilateralism, there are some core principles that characterize multilateralism: a spirit of collectivity, inclusivity over exclusivity and, above all, negotiated governance (D'Alessandra/Gildea 2025: 648). Multilateralism is looked upon as a collective effort of problem-solving. Hence, mutual dialogue, some degree of burden-sharing and partnership are necessary to achieve this. The notion of a collective endeavour also leads actors to prefer the highest degree of inclusivity over exclusivity. The principle of negotiated governance means that states and other stakeholders are willing to seek consensus or reach compromise. This does not exclude power-based bargaining but also permits the exchange of arguments with the possibility of persuading others.

As D'Alessandra and Gilea remind us, the types of multilateralism based on the various principles differ qualitatively (D'Alessandra/Gildea 2025: 649–653) [see Table 2]: Therefore, we can see instances of *formal* multilateralism in which states technically follow the principles cited above. Then their structure of interaction looks collective, however the spirit of collectivity is rather weak, since states pursue their specific interests. Also, inclusivity may actually be rather limited, since participation may be broad but tokenistic. The same applies to negotiated governance, which is only followed minimally, since the rules are only procedural without genuine instances of negotiation. When members show some kind of minimal commitment without real interest in achieving an outcome, this can be called *superficial* multilateralism. The spirit of collectivity is invoked on a rhetorical level, but hardly practised. Participation may seem inclusive, but influence remains with the dominant actors. And as far as negotiations are concerned, their outcomes are often predetermined or shaped by power asymmetries. To qualify as *substantive*, multilateralism must meet high standards on every principle: Interaction must be characterized by a genuine pursuit of common goods beyond self-interest, inclusion must be equitable and participation of all relevant actors meaningful. In addition, negotiations should yield a real compromise based on having identified common interests and on consensus-building with co-created rules.

TABLE 2: The quality of multilateralism depends on adhering to core principles
Types of multilateralism

Core principles / *Type of multilateralism*	Spirit of collectivity	Inclusivity over exclusivity	Negotiated governance
Formal	Weak: structure looks collective, but states often pursue narrow interests	Limited: participation may be broad but tokenistic	Minimal: rules are procedural, little genuine negotiation
Superficial	Rhetorical: invoked in language, but shallow in practice	Mixed: inclusive in appearance, but real influence may remain with dominant actors	Simulated: negotiations occur, but outcomes often predetermined or shaped by power asymmetries
Substantive	Strong: genuine pursuit of common goods, beyond self-interest	Central: meaningful inclusion and equitable participation of all relevant actors	Robust: real compromise, identification of common interests, consensus-building, and co-created rules

Source: Own compilation based on D'Alessandra/Gildea 2025: 648–653.

In reality, we can find instances of all three types of multilateralism in different phases of negotiation processes. In an age of complex multilateralism, in which global cooperation is not only shaped by states, but also by civil-society and private actors like business and philanthropic foundations – traits that underscore the advent of a multiplex order –, reminding us of the core principles of multilateralism helps us understand how the interaction capacity of all stakeholders can be sustained and possibly enhanced. Currently, however, multilateralism and the arenas of multilateral cooperation have become sites not only of open contestation but also of discursively redefining core concepts and rules on which multilateral cooperation used to be based.

3.2 MULTILATERAL COOPERATION IN THE FACE OF GROWING ILLIBERALISM

Only with the abolition of feudalism in the wake of the French Revolution in 1789 did something like electoral autocracies, as we would call them today, start to develop. Democracies as regime type evolved from the mid-19th century onwards, their share steadily increasing after World War I and especially after World War II until about the early 2000s [see Figure 3]. This is why the rise of the system of multilateral institutions we are familiar with is closely linked to democracies and liberal values.

FIGURE 3: Autocracies are on the rise again, coupled with democratic backsliding

Percentage of countries that are democracies or autocracies (World, 1789–2024)

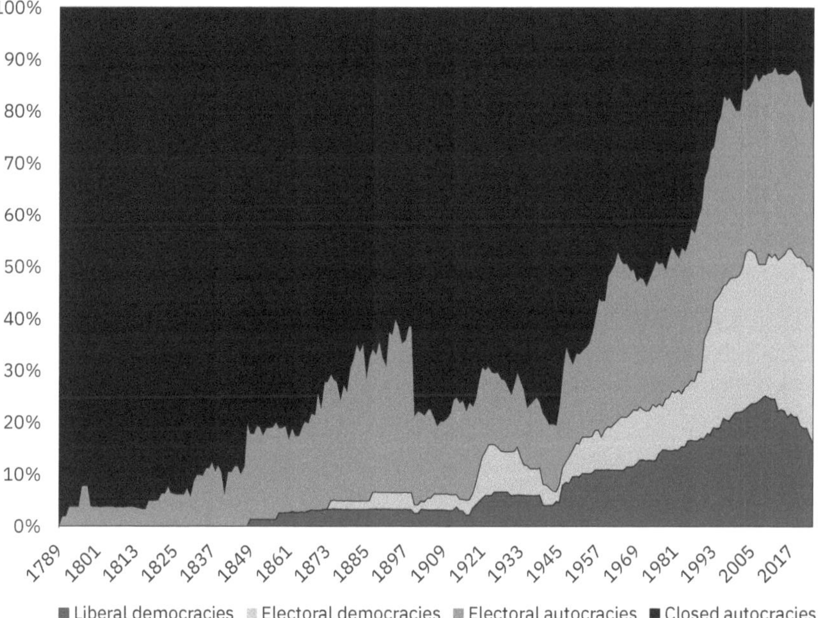

Note: The share of closed autocracies increases a lot in 1900 because V-Dem covers many more countries since then, often former colonies.

Legend:

Closed autocracy: citizens do not have the right to choose either the chief executive of the government or the legislature through multi-party elections.

Electoral autocracy: citizens have the right to choose the chief executive and the legislature through multi-party elections; but they lack some freedoms, such as the freedoms of association or expression that make the elections meaningful, free, and fair.

Electoral democracy: citizens have the right to choose the chief executive and the legislature in meaningful, free and fair, and multi-party elections.

Liberal democracy: electoral democracy and citizens enjoy individual and minority rights, are equal before the law, and the actions of the executive are constrained by the legislative and the courts.

Source: https://ourworldindata.org/democracy; 26.09.2025, data based on the V-Dem Dataset (https://www.v-dem.net/data/the-v-dem-dataset/), regime type classification based on Lührmann/Tannenberg/Lindberg 2018: 62–63.

The historical record reflected in the changing proportions of autocracies and democracies, however, reminds us that norms have always been contested, especially in multilateral institutions with a highly diverse membership. For many years, the liberal character of the international system was safeguarded by the United States as liberal hegemon. But under the auspices of this liberal hegemon the quality of multilateralism also fluctuated from formal to superficial to substantive depending on the respective institution and its decision-making rules, the issue area and the diplomatic craftsmanship of those involved to identify common ground and strike an agreement. Today, substantive multilateralism and the liberal norms enshrined in its core principle of meaningful inclusion and equal participation are under attack. The age of geopolitical power-play seems to have returned, which resonated from the speech of the President of the European Commission cited above.

In fact, there is not only open contestation. On a discursive level, we can witness a more assertive re-interpretation of core concepts like non-intervention and non-interference with reference to national sovereignty. Historically, it is due to the enlarged membership of the UN after several waves of decolonization that also economic and social rights were introduced into the catalogue of human rights. Now, autocratic regimes demand to prioritize economic and social rights over political and civil rights (Cottiero et al. 2025: 244). However, it is not only autocratic states that are becoming more self-confident in multilateral institutions and thus are challenging liberal norms. Currently, in particular the second Trump administration, and also a number of other Western states are also refusing to cooperate in multilateral contexts, citing, for example, that their national sovereignty or social values are at risk (Hooghe/Lenz/Marks 2019). The UN Human Rights Council is especially fertile ground for controversy. There, not only autocratic regimes try to undermine liberal democratic values (Oud 2024). Also states that face democratic backsliding protect autocratic states from normative scrutiny while being more critical against liberal democracies (Meyerrose/Nooruddin 2025).

What we are currently observing is less the end of multilateralism as social institution and means of cooperation, but rather what characterizes the new global multiplex: a world shaped by interdependence, with a diversity of actors and a plurality of norms and values. The question is what principles multilateral cooperation will be based on in the long run, what quality it will have, and if it is able to deliver for people and planet.

4. PROSPECTS AND CHALLENGES FOR MULTILATERAL COOPERATION: THE CONTRIBUTIONS OF THIS BOOK

The signs are quite clear: The liberal international order as we used to know it from the early 1990s on will not return. As the discussion has shown, this may open new avenues of correcting some effects that went with it. The main challenge still lies in reducing inequalities within and between countries and making global decision-making more inclusive – even against the resistance of illiberal states, in which the space for civil society participation is constantly shrinking. We have also learned that so called "norm entrepreneurs" – state or non-state –, who advocate for certain norms, do not always promote only "liberal" or "good" norms. Very often, autocratic and backsliding democratic states are joined by conservative NGOs, when "family values" have to be protected, which usually results in curtailing reproductive rights, in other words: women's rights (Cupać/Ebetürk 2021). Another strategy of illiberal states is to place their citizens in the secretariats of multilateral institutions. China, for instance, uses its growing global engagement strategically to enter the UN civil service (Lam/Fung 2024).

This is the new global context, in which new rules must be negotiated, and old ones (re)interpreted and applied. It also means that on a global level, the pragmatic approach should be to agree on normative guidelines and the goals you want to achieve – and leave the implementation of the policies to the domestic or regional level, as in the case of the Paris Agreement regulating the emission of greenhouse gases. This will not lead to solving problems automatically, as can be seen from the ongoing climate change. However, it makes clear that solving global problems rests on shared – even if differentiated – responsibilities (Ulbert 2018).

The age of interdependence is especially visible with respect to the digital transformation that is under way. The United States and China, conjointly with their big tech companies, dominate digital technologies and services. The new technologies offer both benefits and risks. At UN level, the debate over what rules should shape the transformation and the application of digital technologies is gaining momentum. In her chapter, Cornelia Ulbert argues that we need principles guiding the digital transformation and shows what a human-centred approach can look like and what kinds of regulatory frameworks are currently already in place. Despite digital dependencies on the United States and China, there are ways for states to enhance their digital sovereignty. They do not rest, though, on protective measures but on engaging in producing more global digital public goods.

In a multiplex order, regions are becoming more important. Bringing regions with their wide range of formal and informal institutions into global problem-solving, in his chapter, Christof Hartmann sketches the future of multilateral peace operations with reference to African regional organizations. He shows that the existing international toolbox may still be relevant for stabilizing violent conflicts. The growing regionalization in securing peace contributes to a more pluralist and representative international system in which responsibilities are more widely shared and in which also domestic civil society actors are included, as in the case of infrastructures for peace (see also Fawcett 2025). However, on a global level, the future of multilateral peace operations depends on two crucial factors: The first is the provision of adequate resources. The willingness of the global community to invest in collective security mechanisms would also underline the idea that international peace is a global public good whose costs must be shared. The second factor relates to what kind of peace forthcoming peace operations want to achieve. Stabilization, in essence, just means the absence of violence. The SDGs reflect a broader notion of peace. That would make it necessary to also address the root causes of conflicts and contribute to transforming conflictual relationships on the domestic level into cooperative ones.

Pluralizing the range of actors that shape global policy processes does not only mean that the landscape of actors has become more diverse. One of the consequences is that authority, the power and – if legitimately delegated – also the right to take decisions that have effects on a collective, does not only rest with states anymore. There is much empirical evidence that private actors play a major role in a multitude of international and transnational regulatory processes today, especially relating to global value chains (Cashore et al. 2021). In their chapter, Christian Scheper and Markus Ciesielski scrutinize the politics of due diligence in global value chain regulation. Private regulation does not replace rulemaking by the state. Rather, reflecting the various functions of private actors in political processes, there are highly diverse forms of private, private-public and public regulation which interact with each other to varying degrees. Emanating from a global process, several regional and national state regulations have developed, supplementing private regulations. These state regulations are increasingly contested and are a vivid example of contestation processes that involve states, civil society and private actors. In essence, due diligence regulation is also an expression of a global struggle over corporate accountability, public authority and the regulation of global production.

The last chapter, by Marcus Kaplan, deals with one of the long-term problems that has not been regulated much on a global level to date: water resources are under severe stress due to increasing demands and reduced availability and quality. Therefore, water stress threatens human well-being, development, and, above all, can trigger intra- and interstate conflicts. Water conflicts have been exacerbated since the access to, and provision of water has become a matter of national security. And increasingly, restricting the access to water is used as a weapon against individual groups or neighbouring countries. However, water diplomacy can be a useful tool for conflict transformation if it is based on identifying shared interests and brings together the different perspectives of all relevant stakeholders in an integrative approach.

The following chapters illustrate that the international order has become more pluralistic with more instances of contestation. However, the new multiplex order still has a multitude of instruments and institutions at its disposal on which global cooperation can be based. In particular for tackling long-term and complex problems we need spaces for negotiation, creation and participation that enable us to think about the future, which might be a common at best. This entails considering unorthodox or new perspectives and approaches, as well as doing justice to the diversity and complexity of global politics – in terms of plurality of actors, disparity in values and multiple scales. For liberal democratic states this also means that they should be conscious about the risk of inattention that comes along with leaving the multilateral institutions to illiberal states. The urgent message reads: re-engage with global governance to seek common ground amid difference.

REFERENCES

Acharya, Amitav 2017: After Liberal Hegemony. The Advent of a Multiplex World Order, in: Ethics & International Affairs 31: 3, 271–285.

Acharya, Amitav 2025: The Once and Future World Order. Why Global Civilization Will Survive the Decline of the West, London.

Acharya, Amitav/Estevadeordal, Antoni/Goodman, Louis W. 2023: Multipolar or Multiplex? Interaction Capacity, Global Cooperation and World Order, in: International Affairs 99: 6, 2339–2365.

Appel, Hilary 2024: Competing Narratives of the Russia-Ukraine War. Why the West Hasn't Convinced the Rest, in: Global Policy 15: 4, 559–569.

Birdsall, Andrea 2016: But We Don't Call it 'Torture'! Norm Contestation During the US 'War on Terror', in: International Politics 53: 2, 176–197.

Börzel, Tanja A./Zürn, Michael 2021: Contestations of the Liberal International Order. From Liberal Multilateralism to Postnational Liberalism, in: International Organization 75: 2, 282–305.

Brosig, Malte/Verma, Raj 2024: The War in Ukraine, the Global South and the Evolving Global Order, in: Global Policy 15: 4, 740–745.

Buzan, Barry 2023: Making Global Society. A Study of Humankind Across Three Eras, Cambridge.

Cashore, Benjamin/Knudsen, Jette Steen/Moon, Jeremy/van der Ven, Hamish 2021: Private Authority and Public Policy Interactions in Global Context. Governance Spheres for Problem Solving, in: Regulation & Governance 15: 4, 1166–1182.

Colgan, Jeff D./Keohane, Robert O. 2017: The Liberal Order Is Rigged. Fix It Now or Watch It Wither, in: Foreign Affairs 96: 3, 36–44.

Cottiero, Christina/Hafner-Burton, Emilie M/Haggard, Stephan/Prather, Lauren/Schneider, Christina J. 2025: Illiberal Regimes and International Organizations, in: The Review of International Organizations 20: 2, 231–259.

Cupać, Jelena/Ebetürk, Irem 2021: Backlash Advocacy and NGO Polarization over Women's Rights in the United Nations, in: International Affairs 97: 4, 1183–1201.

D'Alessandra, Federica/Gildea, Ross 2025: Values and Multilateralism in World Politics, in: The British Journal of Politics and International Relations 27: 2, 643–657.

European Commission 2025: 2025 State of the Union Address by President von der Leyen, Strasbourg, 10 September 2025, Speech/25/2053 (https://ec.europa.eu/commission/presscorner/detail/en/SPEECH_25_2053; 09.10.2025).

Fawcett, Louise 2025: The Changing Regional Faces of Peace. Toward a New Multilateralism?, in: Contemporary Security Policy 46: 2, 372–401.

Finnemore, Martha 2009: Legitimacy, Hypocrisy, and the Social Structure of Unipolarity. Why Being a Unipole Isn't All It's Cracked up to Be, in: World Politics 61: 1, 58–85.

Flaherty, Thomas M./Rogowski, Ronald 2021: Rising Inequality as a Threat to the Liberal International Order, in: International Organization 75: 2, 495–523.

Flonk, Daniëlle/Debre, Maria J 2025: Hollow Multilateralism. How Autocracies Contest the Norms and Procedures of International Organizations, in: International Affairs 101: 4, 1463–1482.

Goddard, Stacie E./Krebs, Ronald R./Kreuder-Sonnen, Christian/Rittberger, Berthold 2024: Contestation in a World of Liberal Orders, in: Global Studies Quarterly 4: 2.

Goddard, Stacie E./Krebs, Ronald R./Kreuder-Sonnen, Christian/Rittberger, Berthold 2025: Liberalism Doomed the Liberal International Order. A Less Legalistic System Would Help Protect Democracies, in: Foreign Affairs Juli 28, 2025 (https://www.foreignaffairs.com/united-states/liberalism-doomed-liberal-international-order; 13.08.2025).

Haggard, Stephan/Kaufman, Robert 2021: Backsliding. Democratic Regress in the Contemporary World. Cambridge.

Hale, Thomas 2024: Long Problems. Climate Change and the Challenge of Governing across Time, Princeton.

Hartmann, Christof/Noesselt, Nele 2020 (eds): China's New Role in African Politics. From Non-Intervention towards Stabilization?, Milton.

Hooghe, Liesbet/Lenz, Tobias/Marks, Gary 2019: Contested World Order. The Delegitimation of International Governance, in: The Review of International Organizations 14: 4, 731–743.

Jacobsen, Katja Lindskov/Larsen, Karen Philippa 2023: Liberal Intervention's Renewed Crisis. Responding to Russia's Growing Influence in Africa, in: International Affairs 99: 1, 259–278.

Keohane, Robert O. 1990: Multilateralism. An Agenda for Research, in: International Journal 45: 4, 731–764.

Lam, Shing-hon/Fung, Courtney J. 2024: Personnel Power Shift? Unpacking China's Attempts to Enter the UN Civil Service, in: Global Policy 15: S2, 135–147.

Lorca, Arnulf Becker 2023: Contesting Global Justice from the South. Redistribution in the International Order, in: International Affairs 99: 1, 41–60.

Lührmann, Anna/Tannenberg, Marcus/Lindberg, Staffan I. 2018: Regimes of the World (RoW). Opening New Avenues for the Comparative Study of Political Regimes, in: Politics and Governance 6: 1, 60–77.

Meyerrose, Anna M./Nooruddin, Irfan 2025: Trojan Horses in Liberal International Organizations? How Democratic Backsliders Undermine the UNHRC, in: The Review of International Organizations 20: 1, 125–156.

Oud, Malin 2024: Powers of Persuasion? China's Struggle for Human Rights Discourse Power at the UN, in: Global Policy 15: S2, 85–96.

Pouliot, Vincent 2011: Multilateralism as an End in Itself, in: International Studies Perspectives 12: 1, 18–26.

Riabov, Oleg/Riabova, Tatiana 2014: The Remasculinization of Russia?, in: Problems of Post-Communism 61: 2, 23–35.

Ruggie, John Gerard 1992: Multilateralism. The Anatomy of an Institution, in: International Organization 46: 3, 561–598.

Sachs, Jeffrey D./Lafortune, Guillaume/Fuller, Grayson/Iablonovski, Guilherme 2025: Financing Sustainable Development to 2030 and Mid-Century. Sustainable Development Report 2025, Paris.

Ulbert, Cornelia 2018: In Search of Equity. Practices of Differentiation and the Evolution of a Geography of Responsibility, in: Ulbert, Cornelia/Finkenbusch, Peter/Sondermann, Elena/Debiel, Tobias (eds.): Moral Agency and the Politics of Responsibility, London, 105–121.

United Nations High Commissioner on Human Rights (UNHCR) 2025: Global Trends. Forced Displacement in 2024 (https://www.unhcr.org/global-trends-report-2024; 05.10.2025).

Union of International Associations 2022: Yearbook of International Organizations 2022–2023. Guide to Global Civil Society Networks, Edition 59, Volume 5: Statistics, Visualizations and Patterns, Leiden.

Weiss, Jessica Chen/Wallace, Jeremy L. 2021: Domestic Politics, China's Rise, and the Future of the Liberal International Order, in: International Organization 75: 2, 635–664.

GLOBAL GOVERNANCE FOR SUSTAINABLE DEVELOPMENT

STRENGTHENING A HUMAN-CENTRED TRANSFORMATION: RULES FOR THE DIGITAL WORLD

Cornelia Ulbert

Abstract: The digital transformation is advancing rapidly. For managing the benefits and risks of digital technologies, especially those based on artificial intelligence, the digital world needs rules that must be based on certain principles which are globally acknowledged like inclusivity, fairness, transparency or respect for human rights. On a global level, the United Nations has been shaping a process of furthering digital cooperation, which culminated in the adoption of the "Global Digital Compact" in 2024. This has been accompanied by national and regional initiatives to regulate digital technologies leading to a growing fragmentation of digital governance. At the same time, more and more countries try to assert their "digital sovereignty" to control their own digital infrastructure, data, and technology. However, this is contradicted by the technological dominance of the United States and China and the oligopolies of their leading tech companies. Therefore, this chapter argues for the promotion of global digital public goods to enlarge the selection of digital choices countries can make.

1. INTRODUCTION

When the High-Level Panel on Digital Cooperation, which was appointed by the United Nations (UN) Secretary-General, issued its report "The Age of Digital Interdependence" in 2019, it already predicted that the "speed and scale of change is increasing" and that "the agility, responsiveness and scope of cooperation and governance mechanisms needs rapidly to improve" (High-Level Panel on Digital Cooperation 2019: 6). The actual speed, however, with which especially applications based on artificial intelligence (AI) have developed since, not only raises high expectations of furthering human progress, but it also arouses fear of misuse and deepening social divisions. Therefore, the former "laissez-faire" global governance regime that was applied to providers of digital technologies (Jia/Chen 2022: 291) has come under pressure, since the social impacts of digital platforms and digital technologies, like a growing amount of disinformation and polarization within and between societies or a systematic violation of data privacy, are felt more profoundly than before.

Both the benefits and risks transcend national borders. We can see various models of regulating the development and application of digital technologies globally. However, the ways and principles of how to do this differ, especially between the three main economic contenders, the United States, China, and the European Union (EU). There has been a stark increase in regulating digital technologies, especially AI systems, over the past years, mainly at the national or regional level. Consequently, the term "digital cooperation" was coined to capture "the ways of working together to address the societal, ethical, legal and economic impacts of digital technologies in order to maximize benefits to society and minimize harms" (High Level Panel on Digital Cooperation 2019: 6). In 2020, amidst the COVID-19-pandemic, the UN devised a "Roadmap for Digital Cooperation" (UN 2020), emphasizing that this will be instrumental in achieving the Sustainable Development Goals (SDGs) as a joint multi-stakeholder effort. The UN's work to further digital cooperation culminated in the "Global Digital Compact" that was adopted by the UN General Assembly as part of the "Pact for the Future" in September 2024 (UN 2024). Geopolitical tensions, the growing spread of autocracies combined with the demise of the liberal international order, however, have led to more and more countries and regional players emphasizing their "digital sovereignty", a concept related to regulating digital spaces and strengthening technological autonomy (Lambach/Monsees 2025: 72).

This chapter engages with this trend of a growing fragmentation of digital governance with competing institutional and policy approaches in the face of a general backlash of multilateral cooperation. Nevertheless, for managing the benefits and risks of digital technologies, especially those based on AI, the digital world needs rules that must be based on certain principles which are globally acknowledged like inclusivity, fairness, transparency or respect for human rights. In an age of digital interdependence, however, the exertion of "digital sovereignty" can only be extended beyond the range of economic and political powerful actors when the number of global digital public goods will increase.

2. PRINCIPLES GUIDING THE GLOBAL DIGITAL TRANSFORMATION

The simple fact that digital technologies transcend national borders renders purely national approaches insufficient. Historically, global cooperation on information and communication technologies (ICTs) started with regulating global connectivity issues by providing the necessary infrastructure. This also led to shared standards and securing interoperability, which predominantly fell into the domain of the International Telecommunication Union (ITU) and later, with the advent of digital technologies, other technical bodies like the Internet Corporation for Assigned Names and Numbers (ICANN). Technical compatibility means that networks, devices, and services work across borders and that harmonized frameworks for cross-border data enable, for instance, global supply chains and other economic or social exchanges.

Multilateral cooperation is also needed for two additional reasons: On the one hand, to cope with the risks and harms associated with digital technologies, especially infringements of individual rights, like data privacy violations, or cybersecurity threats, e.g. cyberattacks, cybercrimes and disinformation campaigns. On the other hand, digitalization is also seen as a means to further the achievement of the UN Sustainable Development Goals (SDGs) (Francisco/Linnér 2023). The "SDG Digital Acceleration Agenda", a joint initiative led by ITU and the UN Development Programme (UNDP) expects "game-changing digital solutions [... to] accelerate progress in climate action, education, hunger, poverty and at least 70 per cent of the 169 SDG targets" (ITU/UNDP 2023: 3). For the UN, digital cooperation has to focus on a "human-centred digital transformation" (UN 2023: 6), which is explicitly linked to the 17 SDGs. Moreover, with progress on implementing the SDGs stalling, aligning the digital transformation with the SDGs and environmental sustainability is one of the overarching guiding principles that is also shared, amongst others, by the G20 and the Organization for Economic Co-operation and Development (OECD) (G20 2023, OECD 2021) [see Figure 1].

FIGURE 1: Safeguarding a human-centred digital transformation
Principles guiding the global digital transformation on a normative and operational level

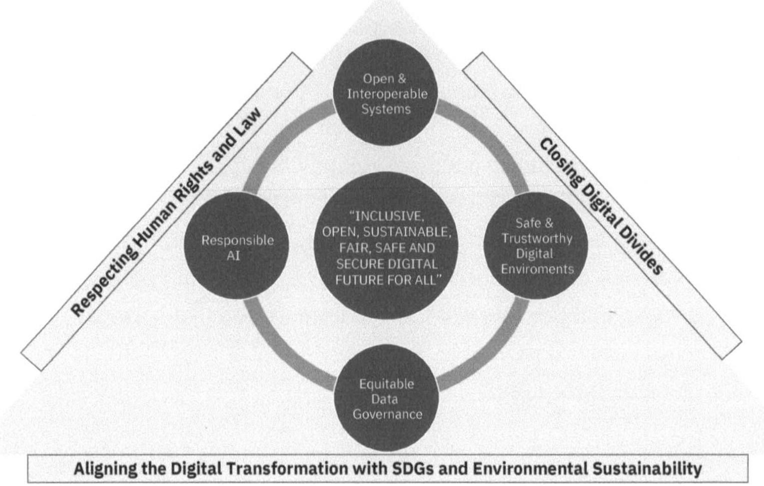

Source: Own compilation.

Since much of the work of UN and other multilateral bodies revolves around norm-setting, safeguarding civil and human rights in the digital age has become one of the most-cited principles in digital cooperation.[1] With the "Framework Convention on Artificial Intelligence", the Council of Europe opened the first-ever international legally binding treaty for signature in September 2024, which "aims to ensure that activities within the lifecycle of artificial intelligence systems are fully consistent with human rights, democracy and the rule of law, while being conducive to technological progress and innovation".[2] According to the UN Global Digital Compact the goal of the current digital transformation should be "an inclusive, open, sustainable, fair, safe and secure digital future for all" (UN 2024: Annex I, Para. 4). The realities of today's global access to information and communication technologies (ICTs), however, still reflect the ongoing digital divide between high-income and low-income countries, when you look at key ICT indica-

1 Besides the UN Global Digital Compact (https://www.un.org/global-digital-compact/en; 14.08.2025) see also the OECD principles for trustworthy AI (https://oecd.ai/en/ai-principles; 14.08.2025).

2 https://www.coe.int/en/web/artificial-intelligence/the-framework-convention-on-artificial-intelligence; 14.08.2025.

tors like internet access [see Figure 2]. This is why ensuring universal and equitable digital access has been ranked highly amongst the list of normative principles. On an operational level, you can summarize various catalogues of principles into four principles that also reflect the historical development of digital technologies. These principles focus on 1) open and interoperable systems, 2) safe and trustworthy digital environments, 3) equitable data governance, and 4) responsible AI.

FIGURE 2: The digital divide is still not closed

Percentage of individuals using the internet for the World and special regions (2005–2024)

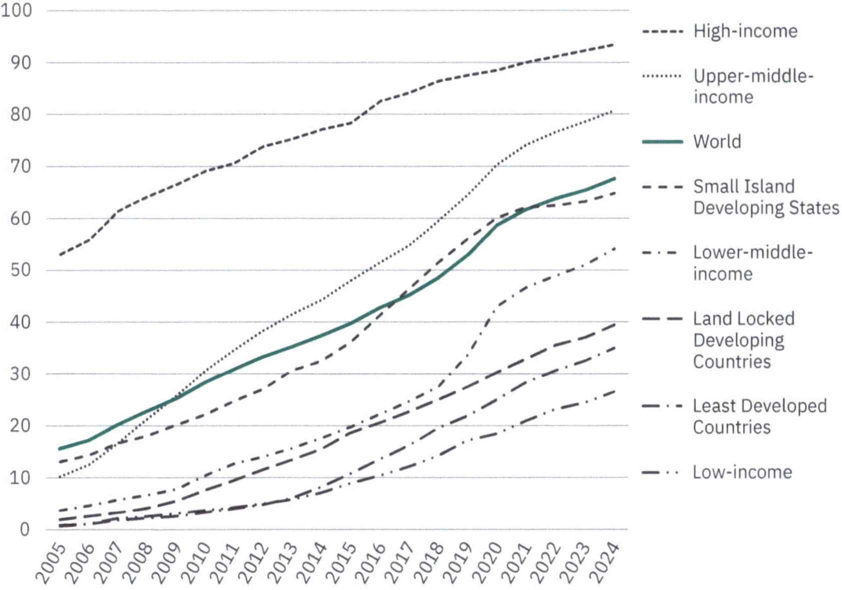

Source: ITU World Telecommunication/ICT Indicators database, version November 2024; https://www.itu.int/en/ITU-D/Statistics/Pages/facts/default.aspx, 11.08.2025.

Open and interoperable systems like the internet are necessary to preserve net neutrality and global digital spaces. Governing the internet has never been a purely technical issue, as the history of the World Summit on the Information Society shows, which led to the creation of the multistakeholder Internet Governance Forum in 2006 as the principal discussion forum on issues of internet governance. To protect users against online harm, misinformation and security challenges it is necessary to create safe and trustworthy digital environments. Many consider data as the most valuable resource that can be mined in the digital age. Hence, the principle of equitable data governance is key to enable privacy-respecting, interoperable, and inclusive use of data. Finally, with the global roll-out of more and more AI-based applications, the question of "responsible AI" has become of utmost importance. This has led the UN Secretary-General's multistakeholder High-Level Advisory Body on Artificial Intelligence to call for "Governing AI for humanity", based on inclusive and risk-based approaches (High-Level Advisory Body on Artificial Intelligence 2024). Although the risks and problems of digital technologies were known before, they have been exacerbated with the rapid development of AI-based application and, subsequently, have resulted in numerous national and multilateral regulations worldwide based on different regulatory approaches (Congressional Research Service 2025).

3. REGULATING RISKS AND PROBLEMS: FRAMEWORKS OF DIGITAL REGULATION

Before the first version of ChatGPT was released in November 2022, the governance of digitalization was widely characterized by an industry-driven, market-based approach with little centralized regulation ("laissez-faire"). With more and more technical, especially AI-based, applications being rolled out globally, it became obvious that not only digital technologies, but also the digital industry itself have to be regulated – to cope with the problems that already were visible and to deal with the emerging risks of the new technologies (Jia/Chen 2022: 287) [see Table 1]. The more so, since a small number of big tech companies (like Alphabet/Google, Amazon, Apple, Meta or Microsoft in the United States and Alibaba, Baidu, Tencent or Huawei in China) have established their global oligopolistic power over data flows, platform technologies, social media, or e-commerce by which they generate not only economic, but also political and cultural power (Bradford 2023: 2). Their economic size and financial wealth allow them to buy any competitor that might threaten their market position, thus contradicting the liberal assumption of competition in free markets (Thumfart 2024: 15). Their wealth also gives them the opportunity to lobby for the kind of (non-)regulation suitable to protect their business models. By the time Elon Musk bought Twitter and transformed it into his political mouthpiece X, it became clear that control over content also meant influence over public discourse. The emergence of more and more AI-based applications has led to a consolidation of big tech power, since they can recruit necessary human resources and they have enough large training datasets and computational power at their disposal (Khanal/Zhang/Taeihagh 2025: 53).

TABLE 1: There is a need for regulating both digital technologies and the digital industry

Technical applications and related problems

	Technical applications	Main problems
Governance of digital technologies	Internet	Global management of Internet Protocol standards
	Artificial intelligence	Externality, ethics, subjectivity, and other risks
	Blockchain	Law lag and malicious use risk
	Algorithm	Rule "black box" and discriminatory risk
	Robotics and automation systems	Decision-making "black box", responsibility risk
	Quantum computing	Data security risk
	Internet of things	Data security risk
	Digital finance technology	Privacy risk and system vulnerability risk
Governance of the digital industry	Digital currency	Legal lag and anti-money laundering risk
	Cross-border data flow	Consistency of data rights protection rules
	Digital tax	Rational distribution of tax base and tax avoidance risk
	Digital platform	Platform power risk
	Sharing economy	Distribution and labour protection
	E-commerce	Intellectual property protection
	Online disinformation	Social and political polarization, erosion of public trust

Source: Jia/Chen 2022: 287 (shortened and adapted version).

The development, deployment, and use of digital technologies and devices involves many resources. Especially so-called generative AI technologies, which can create original content such as text, images, videos, audio, or software code in response to user prompts, leave a considerable larger environmental footprint simply by the amount of computing power, and hence energy that is needed. Therefore AI-based technologies are looked upon as amplifying or exacerbating all the risks that have been associated with individual digital technologies and applications before [see Figure 3]. To cope with these risks, many national and multilateral regulations on AI have been adopted meanwhile. In July 2025 the OECD introduced "GAIIN – the Global AI Initiatives Navigator", a living repository to track public AI policies and initiatives worldwide. When launched, it listed more than 1,300 entries from over 80 jurisdictions and international organizations.[3]

FIGURE 3: AI-based technologies are amplifying existing risks of digital technologies

Current and evolving global risks of AI

Source: UN Chief Executives Board for Coordination 2024: 12.

With respect to their economic weight, three players stand out: the United States, China, and the EU. Interestingly, all follow different regulatory models, which Anu Bradford characterized as different approaches of "digital empires" to shape the global digital order: market-driven (United States), state-driven (China) and rights-driven (EU) (Bradford 2023: 6–11, ch. 1–3) [see Table 2]. As Bradford points out, "the three jurisdictions have all had to balance their support of technological innovation with the implications those technologies have for civil liberties, the

3 https://oecd.ai/en/wonk/introducing-gaiin; 14.08.2025.

distribution of wealth, international trade, social stability, and national security, among other key policy concerns" (Bradford 2023: 7).

During the Biden administration the market-driven approach of the United States had come under scrutiny. However, the current Trump administration has renewed its commitment to relying on a free market with minimalist government intervention, "to develop AI systems free from ideological bias or engineered social agendas".[4] Although there are also growing concerns about the power concentrated in big tech companies and about data privacy in the United States, the Trump administration favours self-regulation by the tech industry and advocates for almost no political regulation. Along these lines, Trump mandated all barriers to AI innovation should be removed to enhance U.S. leadership in AI research and development with the Executive Order issued shortly after his inauguration in January 2025. This is also due to a techno-libertarian view that any government intervention would also undermine individual freedom, exemplified in the emphasis on protecting free speech.

TABLE 2: The United States, China and the EU shaping the global digital order
Three competing regulatory models

Regulatory Model	Core Focus	Governance Style	Mechanism for Global Influence
United States (market-driven)	Free markets, innovation, free speech	Self-regulation, minimal oversight	Tech export, platform dominance
China (state-driven)	State control, stability, technological dominance	Strong government direction	Infrastructure exports, network standards
European Union (rights-driven)	Fundamental rights, rule of law	Rigorous regulation, enforcement	Regulatory diffusion ("Brussels effect")

Source: Own compilation, based on Bradford 2023: ch. 1–3.

China, in contrast, subordinates the digital economy to state control. It encourages technological innovation through active state interventions to maximize the country' technological dominance. The state itself, however, uses digital technol-

4 Executive Order 14179 of January 23, 2025: Removing Barriers to American Leadership in Artificial Intelligence (https://www.federalregister.gov/documents/2025/01/31/2025-02172/removing-barriers-to-american-leadership-in-artificial-intelligence; 15.08.2025).

ogies for censorship and surveillance of its citizens to ensure – from a Chinese point of view – social harmony. The active promotion of Chinese digital infrastructure and technology in countries of the Global South, e. g. through the Digital Silk Road component of its Belt and Road Initiative, invited criticism that China would export digital authoritarianism. However, also non-China based companies have sold their surveillance technologies worldwide (Heeks et al. 2024: 81–83). Remarkably, as Heeks et al. emphasize, "China's digital expansion is not merely technological, but also institutional" (Heeks et al. 2024: 84), since the technology is not only related to informal (management culture, views on human rights) and formal norms (like the choice of currency for economic transactions) but also to formal institutions like regulations and standards.

The EU starts from a similar assumption like the United States, since digital technologies are looked upon as promoting individual liberty and freedom in society. However, in contrast to the United States and China, the EU puts protecting fundamental rights, like data privacy, and preserving the democratic structures of its societies at the centre of its regulatory approach. The human-centric approach of the EU also emphasizes that fair markets are needed, especially to guarantee a fair distribution of the benefits reaped by the digital economy. This also leads to a different conception of the roles of the tech industry and the state, since EU regulation also tries to protect the rights of citizens both towards the tech companies and the state. In terms of influencing the global regulation of digital technologies, however, the rights-based approach of the EU has also been shaping norms beyond its borders, since major firms already preemptively tried to align with its standards, even before the respective regulations entered into force. Or, as was the case with the EU's General Data Protection Regulation (GDPR), big tech companies not only implemented the regulation in the EU but globally, since it saved them adapting their software and services to different jurisdictions with less requirements. This kind of regulatory diffusion is also called the "Brussels effect", which reflects the EU's regulatory power in the global marketplace (Bradford 2023: 324).[5]

With the "Artificial Intelligence Act" (AI Act) the EU acted as norm-setter on AI regulation by establishing a binding comprehensive regulatory and legal framework for the development and use of AI within the EU (Feldstein 2024). It

5 See also Bradford 2020.

came into force in August 2024, with its different degrees of regulation becoming gradually operative within the next 36 months. The AI Act reflects a risk-based regulatory approach that tries to protect the rights of individuals and to ensure that AI systems will do no harm without compromising the tech companies' abilities to innovate.[6] The regulatory instruments which are applied are based on the level of risk which leads to either no specific regulation, information and transparency obligations, conformity assessments or – at the strictest level – the prohibition of certain applications and uses [see Figure 4]. In conjunction with the Framework Convention on Artificial Intelligence of the Council of Europe, the EU AI Act is an important binding regulation in a still weak, but nevertheless existing, regime complex on governing AI with a polycentric structure characterized by many decision centres.[7]

Amidst the different approaches and aspirations of the United States, China, and the EU to shape a global digital order,[8] the UN has instigated a process of countering the fragmentation that has become especially visible in regulating AI. The High-Level Advisory Board on Artificial Intelligence, which was appointed by the UN Secretary-General in October 2023, held several rounds of consultations across stakeholder groups to come up with recommendations on the governance of AI. In the wake of this process, the UN prepared a White Paper on the work of the various bodies and entities of the UN system on AI governance. The focus of this inventory was on the institutional models applied, their related functions, and the normative framework provided by the UN system (UN Chief Executives Board for Coordination 2024: 5).

6 https://artificialintelligenceact.eu/; 14.08.2025.

7 Regime complexes are loosely-coupled sets of specific regime, which are defined as "sets of implicit or explicit principles, norms, rules, and decision-making procedures around which actors' expectations converge in a given area of international relations" (Krasner 1982: 185). For the concept of "regime complex" see Keohane/Victor (2011).

8 For a more extensive analysis of the different approaches of the United States, China and the EU in governing AI see Mokry/Gurol (2024).

FIGURE 4: The risk-based regulatory approach of the EU AI Act
Classifying AI systems into several risk categories with different degrees of regulation applying

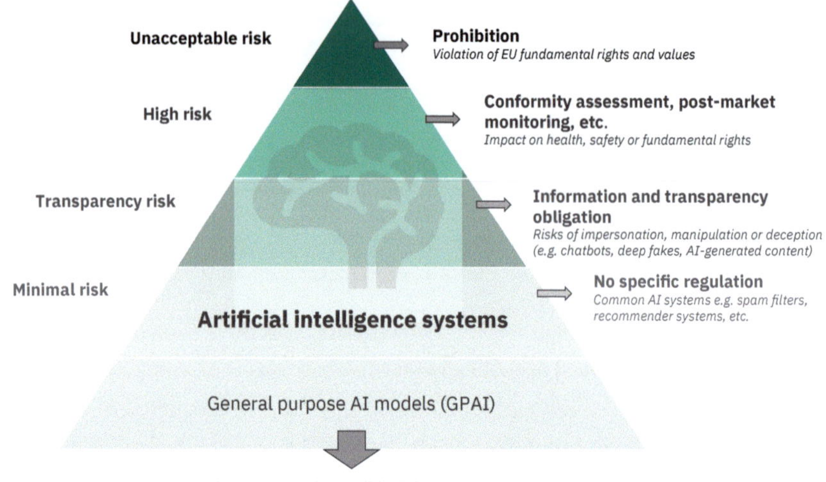

Note: The AI act defines GPAI models as "trained with a large amount of data using self-supervision at scale" and those that display "significant generality" and are "capable to competently perform a wide range of distinct tasks" and "can be integrated into a variety of downstream systems or applications" (Madiega 2024: 7).

Sources: Madiega 2024: 8, Congressional Research Service 2025: 17 (adapted version).

The White Paper identified four key functions the UN system already performs with respect to AI governance: 1) scientific consensus-building, 2) norm-setting, consensus-building around risks and opportunities, 3) regulatory coordination, monitoring, enforcement and 4) development and diffusion of technology (UN Chief Executives Board for Coordination 2024: 15).

In its final report, the High-Level Advisory Board on Artificial Intelligence broke down the different functions into a prospective AI governance architecture emphasizing the role of the UN therein as an "enabling connector" for forging a *common understanding* of AI, finding some *common ground* by initiating a governance dialogue and standards exchange and, above all, reaping *common benefits* by establishing a capacity development network, an AI data framework, and a global fund for AI (High-Level Advisory Body on Artificial Intelligence 2024: 19). The UN General Secretary already submitted a proposal for "Innovative voluntary financing options for artificial intelligence capacity-building" to the UN General

Assembly in July 2025 (UN General Assembly 2025a). The call to create a new international science-driven AI body to forge the desired common understanding was answered by the UN General Assembly in August 2025 by establishing a multidisciplinary "Independent International Scientific Panel on Artificial Intelligence" which is tasked to present its annual report at the "Global Dialogue on AI Governance", a newly created platform for governments and relevant stakeholder "to discuss international cooperation, share best practices and lessons learned" (UN General Assembly 2025b: para. 4).

The question of governing AI on a global level enjoys the highest priority at the UN, since "[t]here is a pressing need to put a floor under the AI divide so as to ensure that the benefits of AI are available to all peoples. This is a critical moment for the building of knowledge, tools and infrastructure, so that no one is left behind in relation to the defining technological revolution of the present decade" (UN General Assembly 2025a: para. 59). The UN's push for closing the AI capacity divide comes at a time when more and more countries talk about strengthening their "digital sovereignty".

4. "DIGITAL SOVEREIGNTY" IN THE AGE OF DIGITAL INTERDEPENDENCE

In a very basic sense "digital sovereignty" refers to the ability of states or organizations to control their own digital infrastructure, data, and technology without undue dependence on or influence from foreign entities. Digital sovereignty is about maintaining (or very often regaining) autonomy in the digital space, which not only comprises digital technologies but also public and private security issues (cyber sovereignty), web content, and internet infrastructure (internet sovereignty), and also touches upon the whole range of data (data sovereignty) and information (information sovereignty) associated with it (Thumfart 2024: 28).

Although the term itself dates back to the 1990s, in the political arena, digital sovereignty became salient when the first Trump administration took a protectionist stance toward China and started banning selected Chinese tech companies from its market (Pohle/Nanni/Santaniello 2024: 666).[9] It was then that China developed its vision of digital sovereignty as a matter of national security further

9 For the historical evolution of the concept and its usage see Thumfart (2024: ch. 3).

and promoted the idea of technological self-reliance, also out of fear of external interference. While building a strong tech industry, the Chinese state also established a comprehensive governmental oversight of data, networks, and digital platforms. Ultimately, the Chinese strategy of promoting its own tech champions has been successful. For instance, within a couple of years, the United States and China became the global leaders in developing AI systems [see Figure 5]. The list of countries, in which AI systems have been developed in recent years, reflects the dependence of most countries on a few high-income and upper-middle income countries, with the exception of India as the only lower-middle income country.

FIGURE 5: United States and China are the global leaders in developing AI systems

Cumulative number of large-scale AI systems by country (2019–2025)

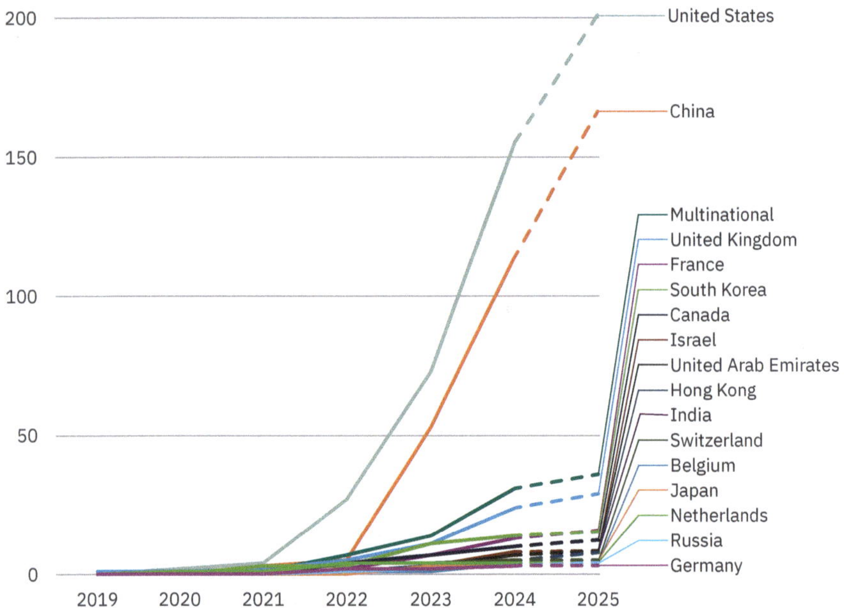

Note: Country refers to the location of the primary organization with which the authors of a large-scale AI system are affiliated. Data for 2025 are incomplete (as of 9 September 2025).

Source: https://ourworldindata.org/grapher/cumulative-number-of-large-scale-ai-systems-by-country; 10.09.2025.

Interestingly, in the face of the technological dominance of the United States and China, European countries also started to resort to the concept of digital sovereignty to assert the self-determination of European states and societies, especially to protect their citizens from violations of data privacy, surveillance and cyber criminality. The adoption of the EU's GDPR in 2016 is looked upon as one critical move in this respect. Therefore, digital sovereignty has become a multidimensional concept addressing not only issues of individual rights and freedoms – as emphasized in the European context – but also collective and infrastructural security problems, questions of political and legal enforceability and, finally, the contentious issue of fair economic competition (Pohle/Nanni/Santaniello 2024: 666).

Much of the current discussions on digital sovereignty are related to economic competitiveness. Some observers think of it as a strategy through which states or supranational entities like the EU try to protect their values and to assert themselves as equal players in a field, in which other actors like the United States, China and globally acting tech firms have taken over leadership (Shahin 2024: 1116). Although the United States, especially now with the second Trump administration, does not seem to be interested in cooperating on issues of digital governance, the second leading tech country, China, actively engages in shaping the discussions in global and regional forums (Heeks et al. 2024: 84–86). Chinese researchers underscore this stance by scientifically arguing for a multi-level governance framework to safeguard digital sovereignty (Qu/Yuan/Xu 2025). The openness of China to engage in norm-setting processes, might contribute to "unthinking digital sovereignty", i.e. reframing the concept, through "debating the procedural frameworks that structure sovereign capabilities and how they can be opened up to public reflection and control" (Pohle/Nanni/Santaniello 2024: 668).

The proposal of the High-Level Advisory Board on AI can help to evolve global digital governance in such a direction. However, this cannot be achieved in a short time. If digital sovereignty means that you are in a position to make choices regarding digital infrastructures, data storage or applications and services – options that are not open to most countries of the Global South –, another strategy would be to enlarge the selection of choices, e.g. by focusing on the provisions of global digital public goods.

5. IN THE FACE OF PENDING GLOBAL DIGITAL GOVERNANCE: PROMOTE GLOBAL DIGITAL PUBLIC GOODS

Digital public goods include open-source software, open data, open AI models, open standards and open content, as specified in many UN documents and reports (see e. g. UNDP 2023). Moreover, as part of a digital public infrastructure, digital identities and registries are becoming increasingly important for social, economic and political participation all over the world. For each type there are already applications available [see Figure 6]. Public goods are characterized by non-rivalry and non-excludability, i. e. if used by one person other persons will still be able to use it, and nobody can be excluded from its usage.

FIGURE 6: Broadening the selection of choices to make "sovereign" decisions
Types of digital public goods and exemplary applications

Open-Source Software	Open AI Models	Open Content
Software with openly available code, free to use, modify and share	AI models that are openly released with permissive licenses	Educational, cultural, or scientific resources freely available to use and adapt
DHIS2 (health data system) KoBoToolbox (data collection in humanitarian crises) OpenMRS (electronic medical records)	BLOOM (multilingual language model) Hugging Face Transformers (natural language processing models)	Wikipedia Khan Academy MIT OpenCourseWare
Open Data	**Open Standards & Protocols**	**Digital Identity & Registries**
Freely accessible datasets for research, policy, and innovation	Agreed technical rules ensuring interoperability and accessibility	Open, secure systems for identity verification and public records
World Bank Open Data NASA Earth Observation Data UN Data Portal	TCP/IP, HTTP (internet protocols) Open311 (civic issue reporting)	MOSIP (Modular Open Source Identity Platform) OpenCRVS (civil registration)

Source: Own compilation, based on the Digital Public Registry of the Digital Public Goods Alliance (https://www.digitalpublicgoods.net/registry; 15.08.2025), Hugging Face (https://huggingface.co/; 15.08.2025).

One global initiative to further the development and application of digital public goods is the "Digital Public Goods Alliance" (DPGA), a multistakeholder partnership of government agencies, international organizations, foundations and open-source platforms (like GitHub). Founded in 2019 as a response to the report "The Age of Digital Interdependence" (High-Level Panel on Digital Cooperation 2019) by iSPIRT, the Indian Software Product Industry Round Table, the governments of Norway and Sierra Leone and the United Nations Children's Fund (UNICEF) (Digital Public Goods Alliance 2023: 8), it is part of an implementation plan of the UN, now under the auspices of the newly created "Office for Digital and Emerging Technologies".[10] The standards developed by DPGA to define if a digital technology conforms to the definition of a digital public good are based on the "Principles for Digital Development",[11] which were developed in the late 2000s in a multi-stakeholder effort originally led by UNICEF.[12] Besides proving the relevance of contributing to achieving the SDGs, and fulfilling some formal requirements like use of approved open licenses, clear ownership, platform independence, documentation and mechanisms for extracting data, there are also some standards that resonate with the principles that are now widely shared in digital governance: the adherence to privacy and applicable laws, the adherence to standards and best practices, and above all, to do no harm by design by respecting data privacy and security, identifying inappropriate and illegal content and protect users from harassment.[13]

Global digital public goods can become a building block in strengthening the weak regime complex for digital global governance, because they contribute to enhancing the digital sovereignty of states and individuals by giving them a choice which digital application or service to use. This makes a vast difference compared to protectionist measures or excluding others from using certain digital tools and hence increases the incentives for cooperation across borders.

6. HOW TO STRENGTHEN GLOBAL DIGITAL GOVERNANCE FOR A HUMAN-CENTRED TRANSFORMATION

There is already a regime complex for global digital governance in existence. It is weak and fragmented, but it gives leeway to cooperate in those formats where progress is possible while others are paralyzed by geopolitical tensions. Moreover, if existing institutions are developed further and better coordinated, they can be useful for governing digital transformation for humanity. The more so since many of the multilateral entities include a diversity of stakeholders, which enhances

10 https://www.un.org/digital-emerging-technologies/content/digital-public-goods; 15.08.2025.

11 https://digitalprinciples.org/; 15.08.2025.

12 https://digitalprinciples.org/; 15.08.2025.

13 https://www.digitalpublicgoods.net/standard; 15.08.2025.

their legitimacy and problem-solving capacity. The current efforts to focus on the governance of AI is a good start, since AI systems encompass and exacerbate all digital risks that have come to the fore and might still arise. Converting the former position of the UN Secretary-General's Envoy on Technology into the position of an Under-Secretary-General and Special Envoy on Digital and Emerging Technologies in the newly established UN Office for Digital and Emerging Technologies has provided an interface and coordinating mechanism within the UN system and contact point with the relevant external stakeholders.[14]

However, some concrete steps would be advisable to develop the global digital governance architecture further:

- **Use the ongoing UN process on global AI governance for engaging in a dialogue:**
  Because of current geopolitical tensions, engaging with countries like China and especially countries of the Global South in various multilateral settings is essential to explore common understandings, common interests and common benefits as envisaged in the newly created AI governance architecture at UN level. With its digital infrastructure, China has exported norms and institutions to many countries of the Global South (Thussu 2025), and the UN process will provide the opportunity to openly discuss the principles and practices guiding the digital transformation, thus also giving lower-middle income and low-income countries a say.

- **Strengthen (regional) efforts of regulatory coordination, monitoring and (possibly) enforcement:**
  The OECD has accumulated a considerable amount of expertise on policies, data and analysis of artificial intelligence. However, it must start to reach out beyond the mainly European members. Together with the Global Partnership on AI and the G20 it could become a focal point of developing frameworks for harmonizing policies, indicators for good governance or recommendations for coping with specific risks (Roberts et al. 2024: 1285).

- **The EU should stick to its rights-based regulatory approach:**
  Despite the threats of U.S. president Trump to sanction the EU with new tariffs, the EU should not back down on enforcing its Digital Markets Act on big tech

14 https://www.un.org/digital-emerging-technologies/; 15.08.2025.

companies like Google as a means of anti-trust regulation. In the same vein, it should not water down the implementation of other digital regulations, like the AI Act, but trust the "Brussels effect", which has already made itself felt with the EU GDPR before, especially since the AI Act is looked upon as a regulatory role model in many countries.

- **Engage in providing global digital public goods and, associated with this, global public digital infrastructures based on widely shared principles and standards:**
  The UN and other – regional – multilateral bodies and multistakeholder initiatives are adequate forums to promote the exchange on the provision of global public goods and discuss and develop the underlying principles and standards further. As always, this will be part of a broader power struggle, but as the history of international negotiations has shown, sometimes it is the power of the better argument that prevails.

REFERENCES

Bradford, Anu 2020: The Brussels Effect. How the European Union Rules the World, Oxford.

Bradford, Anu 2023: Digital Empires. The Global Battle to Regulate Technology, Oxford.

Congressional Research Service 2025: Regulating Artificial Intelligence. U.S. and International Approaches and Considerations for Congress, June 4, 2025, R48555 (https://www.congress.gov/crs-product/R48555; 13.08.2025).

Digital Public Goods Alliance 2023: Digital Public Goods Alliance – 5 Year Strategy. Unlocking the Potential of Open-Source Technologies for a More Equitable World, November 15, 2023 (https://www.digitalpublicgoods.net/dpga-strategy2023-2028.pdf; 15.08.2025).

Feldstein, Steven 2024: Evaluating Europe's Push to Enact AI Regulations. How will this Influence Global Norms?, in: Democratization 31: 5, 1049–1066.

Francisco, Marie/Linnér, Björn-Ola 2023: AI and the Governance of Sustainable Development. An Idea Analysis of the European Union, the United Nations, and the World Economic Forum, in: Environmental Science & Policy 150, 103590.

G20 2023: G20 2023 Action Plan on Accelerating Progress on the SDGs, Varanasi Development Ministerial Meeting, 12 June 2023 (https://g20.utoronto.ca/2023/G20_2023_Action_Plan_for_SDG.pdf; 14.08.2025).

Heeks, Richard, et al. 2024: China's Digital Expansion in the Global South. Systematic Literature Review and Future Research Agenda, in: The Information Society 40: 2, 69–95.

High-Level Advisory Body on Artificial Intelligence 2024: Governing AI for Humanity. Final Report, New York.

High-Level Panel on Digital Cooperation 2019: The Age of Digital Interdependence. Report of the UN Secretary-General's High-Level Panel on Digital Cooperation, New York.

International Telecommunications Union (ITU)/United Nations Development Programme (UNDP) 2023: SDG Digital Accelerator Agenda (https://www.sdg-digital.org/accelerationagenda, 12.08.2025).

Jia, Kai/Chen, Shaowei 2022: Global Digital Governance. Paradigm Shift and an Analytical Framework, in: Global Public Policy and Governance 2: 3, 283–305.

Keohane, R. O./Victor, D. G. 2011: The Regime Complex for Climate Change, in: Perspectives on Politics 9: 1, 7–23.

Khanal, Shaleen/Zhang, Hongzhou/Taeihagh, Araz 2025: Why and How is the Power of Big Tech Increasing in the Policy Process? The Case of Generative AI, in: Policy and Society 44: 1, 52–69.

Krasner, Stephen D. 1982: Structural causes and regime consequences: regimes as intervening variables, in: International Organization 36: 2, 185–205.

Lambach, Daniel/Monsees, Linda 2025: Beyond Sovereignty as Authority. The Multiplicity of European Approaches to Digital Sovereignty, in: Global Political Economy 4: 1, 71–88.

Madiega, Tambiama 2024: Artificial Intelligence Act. Briefing – EU Legislation in Progress, European Parliamentary Research Service, PE 698.792, September 2024 (https://www.europarl.europa.eu/RegData/etudes/BRIE/2021/698792/EPRS_BRI(2021)698792_EN.pdf; 13.08.2025).

Mokry, Sabine/Gurol, Julia 2024: Competing Ambitions Regarding the Global Governance of Artificial Intelligence. China, the US, and the EU, in: Global Policy 15: 5, 955–968.

Organization for Economic Co-operation and Development (OECD) 2021: Development Co-operation Report 2021: Shaping a Just Digital Transformation, Paris.

Pohle, Julia/Nanni, Riccardo/Santaniello, Mauro 2024: Unthinking Digital Sovereignty. A Critical Reflection on Origins, Objectives, and Practices, in: Policy & Internet 16: 4, 666–671.

Qu, Runze/Yuan, Yuhang/Xu, Jinghong 2025: Pathways to Safeguarding Digital Sovereignty Within a Multi-Level Governance Framework. A Cross-National Comparative Study Based on the FsQCA Method, in: Policy & Internet 17: 3, e70009.

Roberts, Huw/Hine, Emmie/Taddeo, Mariarosaria/Floridi, Luciano 2024: Global AI Governance. Barriers and Pathways Forward, in: International Affairs 100: 3, 1275–1286.

Shahin, Jamal 2024: Dancing to the Same Tune? EU and US approaches to Standards Setting in the Global Digital Sector, in: Journal of European Integration 46: 7, 1111–1131.

Thumfart, Johannes 2024: The Liberal Internet in the Postliberal Era. Digital Sovereignty, Private Government, and Practices of Neutralization, Cham.

Thussu, Daya Kishan 2025: China's Deepening Digital Presence in the Global South, in: The Round Table 114: 4, 363–378.

UN Chief Executives Board for Coordination 2024: United Nations System White Paper on Artificial Intelligence Governance. An Analysis of Current Institutional Models and Related Functions and Existing International Normative Frameworks within the United Nations System that are Applicable to Artificial Intelligence Governance (UN Doc. CEB/2024/1/Add.1), New York.

United Nations (UN) 2020: Roadmap for Digital Cooperation. Report of the Secretary-General, June 2020, New York (https://www.un.org/en/content/digital-cooperation-roadmap/assets/pdf/Roadmap_for_Digital_Cooperation_EN.pdf; 12.08.2025).

United Nations (UN) 2023: Our Common Agenda. Policy Brief 5: A Global Digital Compact. An Open, Free and Secure Digital Future for All, New York (https://digitallibrary.un.org/record/4011891?v=pdf; 11.08.2025).

United Nations (UN) 2024: Pact for the Future. Global Digital Compact and Declaration on Future Generations (UN Doc. A/RES/79/1), New York.

United Nations (UN) General Assembly 2025a: Innovative Voluntary Financing Options for Artificial Intelligence Capacity-Building. Report of the Secretary-General (UN Doc. A/79/966), New York.

United Nations Development Programme (UNDP) 2023: Digital Public Goods for the SDGs. Emerging Insights on Sustainability, Replicability & Partnerships; New York (https://www.undp.org/publications/digital-public-goods-sdgs; 15.08.2025).

United Nations (UN) General Assembly 2025b: Terms of Reference and Modalities for the Establishment and Functioning of the Independent International Scientific Panel on Artificial Intelligence and the Global Dialogue on Artificial Intelligence Governance. Draft Resolution Submitted by the President of the General Assembly (UN Doc. A/79/L.118), New York.

PEACE AND SECURITY

FROM LIBERAL PEACE TO STABILIZATION? THE FUTURE OF MULTILATERAL PEACE OPERATIONS

Christof Hartmann

Abstract: As the world is entering a phase of heightened geopolitical tensions, with open military conflicts in Europe, Asia, and Africa, the UN-led multilateral peacekeeping regime is more contested than ever, amid a wider crisis affecting UN finances and legitimacy. At the same time, it remains widely appreciated for its central role and historical record in managing a number of protracted violent conflicts. The liberal approach which had guided most multilateral peace operations since the early 1990s has lost much of its appeal, and two trends have thus shaped UN peace operations throughout the last decade: a growing concern with stabilization, and a growing number of regional organizations involved in such operations. While we observe a trend towards unilateral interventionism, UN policymakers seem divided between those who want to save peacekeeping through a pragmatic approach, orchestrating the activities of different actors with different mandates and rationales, and those which defend the broader idea of multilateral peacebuilding integrating a variety of military and non-military instruments.

1. INTRODUCTION

Over the last three decades, a system of international peacekeeping has emerged, centred around the United Nations (UN) as the global institution mandated to secure international peace and security. UN peace operations were contested from the beginning, for their apparent narrow focus on securing a more limited or "negative" peace, for the bureaucratic, top-down and cost-intensive procedures, and for the selectivity in addressing violent conflicts around the globe. As the world is now entering a phase of heightened geopolitical tensions, with open military conflicts even in those parts of the world which had benefitted from a long absence of war and related mass killings, we might better appreciate the efforts and merits of the loose multilateral peacekeeping regime which has been established since the early 1990s, and which is now questioned, amidst a larger crisis affecting UN finances and legitimacy.

The peacekeeping model has relied not only on the UN but a variety of regional security arrangements to establish peacekeeping missions in their respective regions. Discourses about the decline of the rule-based multilateral order do not refer only to open violations of international law (such as military attacks on the territory of sovereign states) but also to the relevance of international institutions for preventing violent conflicts and for managing those which have erupted in line with some core normative principles and as a joint task for the international community.

The crisis of multilateralism is also a crisis of multilateral peace operations. Unfortunately, the decrease of major UN multidimensional peace operations has been accompanied by an increase in violent conflicts worldwide during the 2010s [see Figure 1]. The demand for multilateral peace operations is thus greater than ever. Therefore, the chapter will make a case for a continued and sustained support for international peacekeeping. The future of multilateral peace operations might thus consist in a better coordinated division of labour between global and regional actors as well as in a stronger appreciation of a variety of non-military instruments of peace operations.

The rise of UN peacekeeping started in the 1990s, and the chapter will reconstruct key developments before discussing two major trends which have characterized the last decade, peace operations with the main goal of stabilization, as well as a regionalization of such operations. We will then conclude by sketching three different scenarios for future peace operations.

FIGURE 1: The dynamics of peace missions and violent conflicts
Number of active UN peacekeeping operations in comparison to number of violent state-based conflicts (1979–2024)

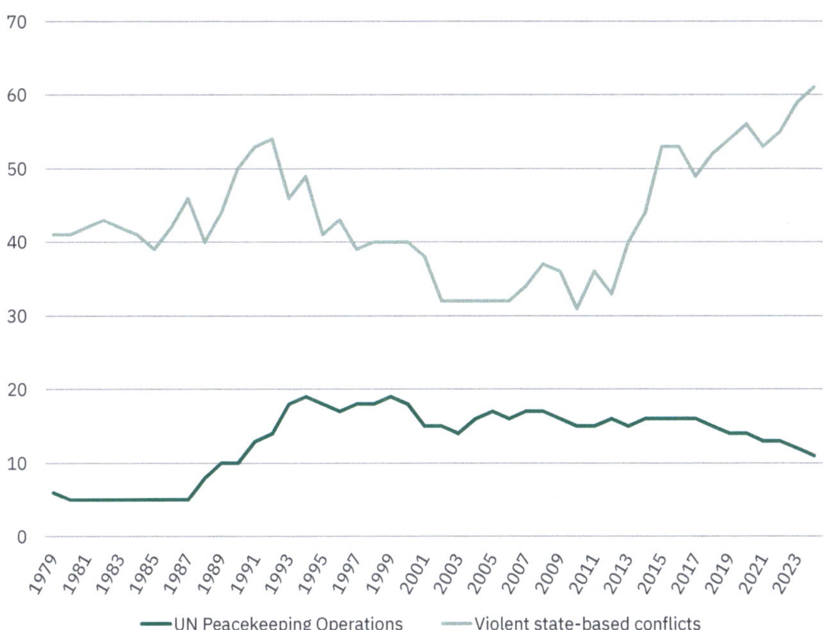

Source: Own compilation based on Hellmüller/Pinaud/Lanfranchi 2025, Davies et al. 2025: 1226 (UCDP/PRIO Armed Conflict Dataset version 25.1, https://ucdp.uu.se/downloads/index.html#armedconflict; 05.09.2025).

2. THE UN AS CENTRAL ACTOR IN MULTILATERAL PEACEKEEPING

While multilateral peace operations have been authorized by a variety of international organizations, the UN peace operations remain at the centre of all major political, conceptual, and normative debates about international peacekeeping. Since their inception in the late 1940s, UN peace operations have evolved in response to novel global political dynamics and changing conflict constellations. Initially focused on monitoring ceasefires and maintaining peace between warring states (peace*keeping*), during the last three decades the role of UN peace operations has expanded to include a much broader array of functions aimed at supporting sustainable peace across the entire conflict cycle, including in the midst of active armed conflicts. Until the end of 2024, the UN had deployed over 120 peace operations in more than 50 countries (Wane/Williams/Kihara-Hunt 2024: 4).

FIGURE 2: The heyday of UN peacekeeping missions is over
Number of newly launched peacekeeping operations and special political missions per year (1946–2024)

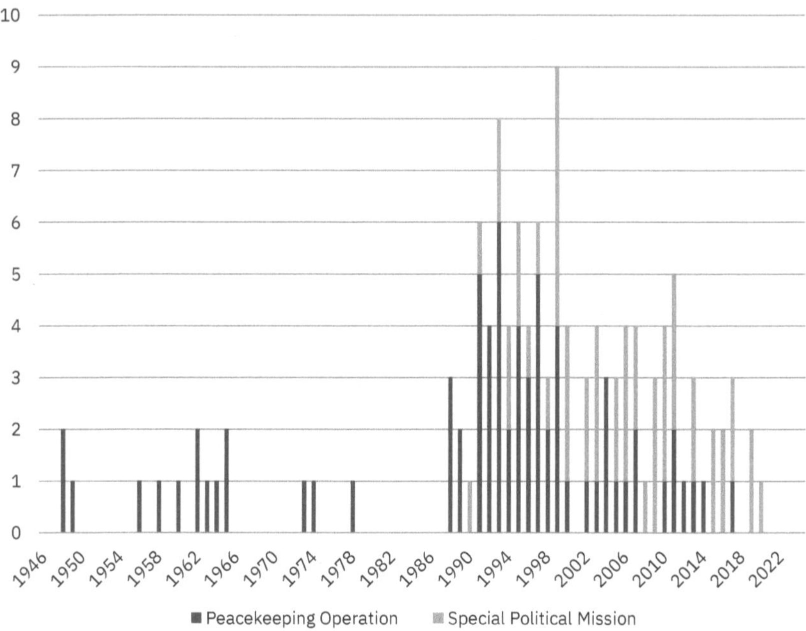

Source: Wane et al. 2024: 8 (adapted version).

Since the 1950s, UN peacekeeping has been guided by the three key principles of impartiality, consent, and the non-use of force. As a core norm of peacekeeping, impartiality prescribed that UN officials should be unbiased when making decisions and particularly so in implementing their mandate. The main parties to a conflict should consent to peacekeeping, and UN peace missions should not use force, except in self-defence (and in defence of the mandate). Between 1948 and the end of 1980s, these principles were upheld, but few peacekeeping operations were newly established [see Figure 2]. UN missions need to be authorized by the UN Security Council, and during the Cold War the two super-powers, United States and the (then) Soviet Union, used their veto to block any UN involvement in dealing with violent conflicts and peace settlements in areas of strategic interest to them, so that a range of major conflicts could not be handled through UN peace missions. Nevertheless, in 1988, UN peacekeepers were awarded the Nobel Peace Prize.

The end of the Cold War offered a window of opportunity for making the UN a more substantial and encompassing peace actor. The idea of attributing the UN a more prominent role in international efforts to manage violent conflicts did no longer face principled opposition within the UN Security Council. The demise of the global bipolar system also provoked a range of violent conflicts in Eastern Europe and parts of Africa and Asia over the control of state power and resource flows. International peace and stability seemed now to be less threatened by inter-state war than by intra-state conflicts and civil wars. In this context, the Agenda for Peace tabled by UN Secretary-General Boutros-Ghali in 1992 claimed a comprehensive and active role for the UN in stabilizing this post-Cold War world. The UN mandate should thus cover the entire conflict cycle, laying out concepts and strategies for *preventive diplomacy*, *peacemaking* and *peacekeeping*, as well as *peacebuilding*, considered at the time as post-conflict efforts to strengthen and solidify peace (Boutros-Ghali 1992). The Agenda for Peace represents the first conceptual step in the evolution of UN thinking on peacebuilding and peace operations [see Figure 3].

While the military remained the backbone of UN peace operations, they were thus incrementally turned from restricted observational missions to multidimensional interventions, combining "keeping the peace" with restructuring of security sectors (through disarmament, demobilization, and reintegration), supervising elections, promoting human rights, reconciliation, and at times also assuming civilian administrative roles. According to this new UN thinking, sustainable peace would be created through the (re)construction of liberal post-conflict political orders. Between 1989 and 1994, the UN Security Council authorized 20 new operations, among them securing complex peace agreements in Angola, Cambodia, El Salvador, Mozambique, and Namibia, thus increasing the number of blue helmets from 11,000 to 75,000.[1] UN peace missions were also established in

1 United Nations Peacekeeping: Our History, https://peacekeeping.un.org/en/our-history; 28.08.2025.

former Yugoslavia, Rwanda, and Somalia, yet these three operations dramatically revealed the limits of UN peacekeeping in contexts of ongoing violent conflict.

The new volatile contexts and more hostile environments represented a major challenge to the key principles of UN peacekeeping. Independent inquiries into UN actions during the 1994 genocide in Rwanda and a UN Secretary-General report into the events of Srebrenica stressed the imperative for the UN to protect civilians. Within UN doctrines, starting with the Brahimi Report of 2000 (UN 2000), a shift occurred from a passive to a proactive conception of impartiality which requested UN missions in particular to protect civilians and human rights, irrespective of whether non-state actors or elements of the state apparatus posed a threat to civilians. Since then, protecting civilians is a standard element of peacekeeping mandates, yet UN contingents often lack the military resources required to prevent attacks on the people they are supposed to protect. While the principle of non-use of force might have been relaxed, in practice the use of deadly force, particularly in a proactive or preventive manner, remains a relatively rare occurrence (Duursma et al 2023: 420). In fact, during the more recent UN operations in the Democratic Republic of the Congo (DRC) and Central African Republic, local populations even launched protests against the UN missions there for their failure to proactively fight rebel groups. The third peacekeeping principle, i. e. the main conflict parties' consent to peacekeeping, has also been modified over time, and was increasingly understood as consent of the host state within post-1990s missions deployed in intra-state wars.

The main lesson drawn from failures in Bosnia and Rwanda was not to reduce ambitions, but to upscale, and to move towards more complex and multidimensional missions, centred on protecting civilians, but also seeking to contribute to longer-term peace- and state-building. In East Timor (UNTAET) and Kosovo (UNMIK), the UN served as de facto authority of would-be independent new states. In 2000, UN Security Council also approved resolution 1325 formally establishing the Women, Peace, and Security Agenda, which required UN peace operations to integrate gender relations into their mandates. In the following years, the UN Security Council authorized additional major peacekeeping operations, especially in Africa, such as in Burundi (2004), Chad and Central African Republic (2007), Côte d'Ivoire (2004), Liberia (2003), as well as several missions in Sudan and South Sudan (2005, 2007, 2011). Outside Africa, new missions were established briefly in Syria (2012) and Haiti (2004). Traditional observer peacekeeping missions in the Middle East (1948), Jammu/Kashmir (1949), Cyprus (1964), and the Western Sahara (1991) were also maintained.

FIGURE 3: The evolution of UN thinking on peacebuilding and peace operations

Key UN documents on peacebuilding

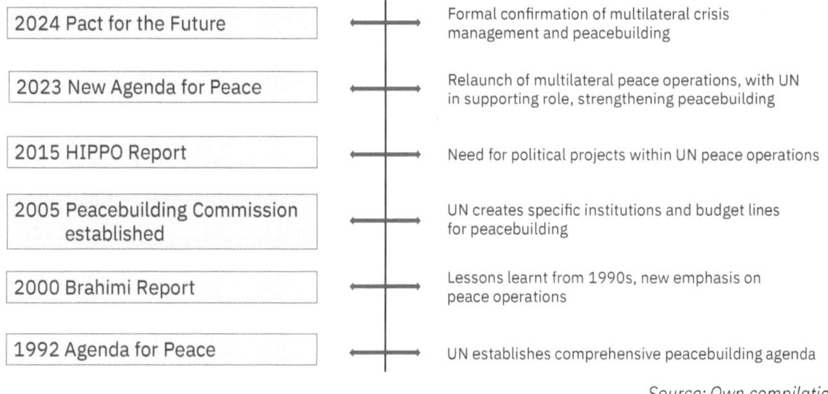

Source: Own compilation.

3. CHANGING PRACTICE: TOWARDS STABILIZATION MISSIONS

Despite many setbacks, most of these UN missions helped end insurgencies, backstop elections and provide political stability in countries including Liberia and Côte d'Ivoire. Research has established that most of these missions were considered successful (Walter/Howard/Fortna 2021). Assessment of the UN missions were however overshadowed by the disastrous non-UN-led interventions in Iraq and Afghanistan. Yet, the UN multidimensional peace operations which were eventually deployed to Mali and Central African Republic (MINUSMA 2013, MINUSCA 2014), took over the stabilization agenda which had characterized the Western-led intervention in Afghanistan. In fact, the four missions in Mali, Central African Republic, DRC and Haiti were authorized with the explicit mandate to stabilize countries in which no peace agreements had been reached yet, mandated with protecting civilians and governments against an aggressor or general destabilization, amidst ongoing violence, while at the same time being part of a larger process that seeks a political settlement for the conflict.

The overall number of UN (military, police and civilian) peacekeepers had gradually increased to a record level of 126,247 by April 2015, but since 2014 no major UN peacekeeping operation has been established, and the UN also closed some larger operations in Côte d'Ivoire, Darfur, Haiti, Liberia, and more recently, Mali. By May 2025, 11 peacekeeping operations were still active (with a total of 68,784 peacekeepers),[2] with the remaining three large missions (DRC, Central African Republic, South Sudan) in the process of further downsizing. Instead of UN peacekeeping operations, the UN Security Council has deployed Special Political Missions (SPMs) which employ political and diplomatic instruments to promote peace, yet typically cannot protect civilians due to lack of military units.

The gradual "uploading" of stabilization into UN practice (Curran/Hunt 2020: 51) reflected both a changing international context and increasing consensus among members of the UN Security Council to mandate robust operations to contain aggressors and spoilers in the midst of conflict, as well as the different type of conflict theatres where it was impossible to stick to traditional notions of peacekeeping. The turn towards stabilization had several problematic effects which explain its meagre popularity within UN bureaucracy, but also the lack of major diplomatic protest, when Mali effectively decided in 2023 not to extend the UN peace operation.

We need first to consider what de Coning (2023: 157) has called the stabilization dilemma. The more effectively a peace operation protects civilians and helps to achieve stability, the less incentive there is for ruling political elites to find long-term political solutions. All parties somehow assume that the state is likely to collapse, or to lose significant parts of its territory to armed groups, should the peacekeeping operation withdraw. As a result, the Security Council keeps these operations in place without a proper exit-strategy. Although all these operations are tasked with mediation and good offices mandates, it has, second, proven more and more difficult to promote a political project for sustaining peace. The respective governments have tried to limit the political role the UN mission might play, and "non-state armed groups may not necessarily see the UN as an honest broker if it has engaged in stabilization actions against them" (Duursma et al. 2023: 438). The Report of the High-Level Independent Panel on Peace Operations (HIPPO Report) in 2015 stressed the "primacy of politics", emphasizing that UN peacekeeping operations can be effective only when there is a viable political project they can support and protect:

2 See https://peacekeeping.un.org/en/data; 28.08.2025.

> “Lasting peace is not achieved nor sustained by military and technical engagements, but through political solutions. The primacy of politics should be the hallmark of the approach of the United Nations to the resolution of conflict, during mediation, the monitoring of ceasefires, assistance to the implementation of peace accords, the management of violent conflicts and longer-term efforts at sustaining peace” (UN 2015a, para 43).

Third, while earlier generations of UN operations were criticized for the heavy emphasis on the external engineering of liberal transformation, stabilization missions tended to turn into illiberal regime-supporting operations, with UN reluctant to call out government abuses for fear of straining relations, and in the process even undercutting long-term bottom-up efforts to build peace. According to Paris (2024: 2170) UN practice has tended towards an “authoritarian peacebuilding model” which tends to empower coercive states most of the time.

4. MORE THAN COMPLEMENTARY: THE RISE OF REGIONAL PEACE OPERATIONS

The slow demise of UN peacekeeping is not tantamount to the end of multilateral peace missions. While the UN Charter reserves the UN Security Council monopoly on legitimately launching peace operations, other international organizations have either been delegated this right by the Security Council or sometimes ignored this rule in practice, and the number of regional organizations emerging as recognized peacekeepers increased since the end of the Cold War. This evolution reflects both an activation of the original division of labour within the UN Charter, but was also a reaction to the shrinking support of Westerns states to UN peace operations since the mid-1990s. Regional organizations thus offered the only available conflict management responses to ongoing civil wars (Coleman/Williams 2021: 248), although some parts of the world have apparently solved conflicts without multilateral peace operations (Bastaki/Staniland/Popoola 2024).

FIGURE 4: Number of African-led missions surpasses UN missions active on the African continent

Number of UN, African-led and hybrid missions in Africa (2011–2022)

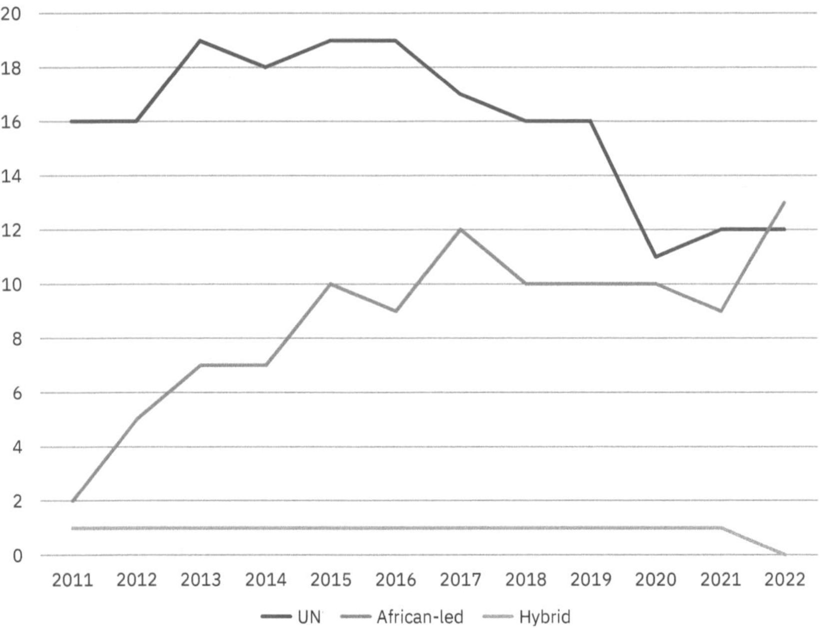

Source: Witt/Hartmann/Engel 2026: 4.

While the UN has not deployed new military peacekeeping operations since 2014,[3] more than ten such missions have been started by other organizations in Africa alone. This category combines both official peacekeeping missions by regional organizations but also ad hoc missions, such as the Multinational Joint Task Force Accra Initiative (MNJTF-AI) to fight terrorism in West African countries. Compared to UN missions, ad hoc coalitions can be established on relatively short notice to deal with a specific crisis situation, and might still mobilize funding from the EU and other actors if endorsed by the UN Security Council or a regional organization like the African Union's (AU) Peace and Security Council (Coleman/Williams 2021: 248). In 2024, the number of African-led missions has surpassed UN missions active on the African continent for the first time [see Figure 4]. Globally, the UN,

3 An exception is the UN Mission in Haiti (2017–2019), considered as Peacekeeping Operation by the dataset used in this chapter.

however, still has more peacekeepers on the ground than all other organizations together [see Figure 5].

FIGURE 5: The UN still deploys the highest number of peacekeeping personnel worldwide

Number of international personnel in multilateral peace operations, by type of conducting organization (2017–2024)

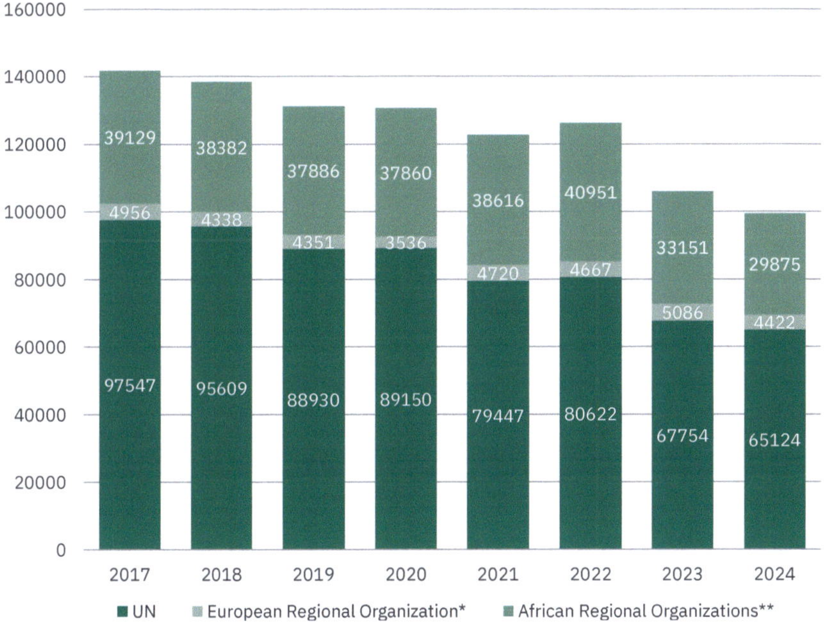

* **European Regional Organizations:** European Union (EU), Organization for Security and Co-operation in Europe (OSCE)

** **African Regional Organizations:** African Union (AU), Economic Community of West African States (ECOWAS), Southern African Development Community (SADC), Intergovernmental Authority on Development (IGAD), East African Community (EAC), Lake Chad Basin Commission (LCBC) and Group of Five for Sahel (G5 Sahel)

Source: Own compilation based on SIPRI Maps of Multilateral Peace Operations 2018–2025.
https://www.sipri.org/sites/default/files/2018-06/mpo18.pdf; 08.09.2025
https://www.sipri.org/sites/default/files/2019-05/mpo19_0.pdf; 08.09.2025
https://www.sipri.org/sites/default/files/2020-06/mpo20_fill.pdf; 08.09.2025
https://www.sipri.org/sites/default/files/2021-05/mpo21_final.pdf; 08.09.2025
https://www.sipri.org/sites/default/files/2022-05/mpo22.pdf; 08.09.2025
https://www.sipri.org/sites/default/files/2023-05/mpo23_3.pdf; 08.09.2025
https://www.sipri.org/sites/default/files/2024-05/mpo24_web.pdf; 08.09.2025
https://www.sipri.org/sites/default/files/2025-05/mpo25_1.pdf;08.09.2025

Regional peace operations had originally been conceptualized as being complementary, but also subsidiary to UN peace operations. This is also the logic of the UN Charter with its separation of Chapter VII and VIII. Several key UN documents of the last decade have however moved from thinking entirely in terms of subsidiarity towards greater "partnership peacekeeping" (UN 2015b). The New Agenda for Peace puts strong emphasis on regional operations as "critical building blocks for the networked multilateralism envisaged" (UN 2023: 12) and UN support to these rather than deploying UN peacekeeping operations as such. As more "robust" UN operations seem to challenge principles and exceed capabilities, regional operations might be the solution for maintaining multilateral peacekeeping.

Evidence concerning such partnerships shows that over the last two decades the UN-EU partnership has lost most of its operational relevance and turned towards a more political relationship. The EU served as an exit strategy for the UN in Bosnia and in Chad. At the UN's request, it has additionally undertaken short-term military stabilization operations in the DRC and Central African Republic (Duursma et al. 2023: 450). With the EU now concentrating on training and capacity building missions in Europe, Middle East, Caucasus, and Africa, its relationship to the UN has become less crucial. Much more critical is the evolution of cooperation between UN and African regional organizations, particularly the AU. Since the creation of the African Peace and Security Architecture (APSA) in 2002, around 40 African-led peace operations have been launched (Duursma et al. 2023: 450), with the majority led by the AU, but also by the regional economic communities (RECs) (such as the Economic Community of West African States (ECOWAS)) and ad hoc coalitions (such as the G5 Sahel Joint Force). We thus observe an increasing heterogeneity of African peace operations. The APSA was built on the assumption that RECs serve as pillars of a continental framework with the AU coordinating and mandating peace operations. In practice, there is a relatively strong fragmentation and overlap, and the ad hoc coalitions might weaken the legitimacy of the formal structures established two decades ago.

Regional peace operations might be more likely candidates for robust mandates and peace enforcement, as they can have different rules defining peacekeeping than the traditional UN principles of impartiality and non-use of force. Based on their founding treaties and additional protocols, both AU and ECOWAS might mandate peace operations which do not require the consent of the main conflict parties or the minimum use of force. Regional and ad hoc coalitions might also offer a legal and political alternative to UN peace operations with less emphasis on human rights, international humanitarian law, and protection of civilians. Some ad hoc interventions have failed to get international recognition as peace operations, such as the Southern African Development Community intervention in DRC (1998), or the U. S.-led invasion of Iraq (2003).

The most problematic aspect of "partnership" peacekeeping has been the trend of some African host governments turning to additional security "partners" with UN missions still active on their territories. Both the governments of Central African Republic (2017) and Mali (2022) invited Russian private security providers into their country, sometimes active in the same areas as UN missions, and partly entering into conflict with UN officials. In 2022, the DRC government invited a coalition of East African countries to deploy a peace enforcement mission in the eastern DRC to combat rebel movements that the UN had failed to defeat, before requesting in 2024 an intervention by Southern African counterparts to escalate operations in the east. In both cases, there was little idea of how these various coalitions would cooperate with the UN mission (Gowan/Forti 2023). Host communities might also no longer be able to distinguish between the UN and parallel forces, or actions undertaken by a partner mission might erode the UN's credibility and legitimacy, with implications for the security of its peacekeepers. There are, however, also more benign forms of collaboration arrangements. In the past, French military contingents cooperated with UN missions in Côte d'Ivoire or Mali, and small EU missions have supported a much larger UN mission, or bolstered UN response in critical situations (such as in DRC 2003 and 2006).

5. THE FUTURE OF MULTILATERAL PEACE OPERATIONS – THREE SCENARIOS

In many ways, the structural environment for multilateral peacekeeping has thus changed. With a divided UN Security Council and lingering support among UN leadership and within member states, the UN is unlikely to return any time soon to multidimensional peace operations with robust mandates, although a minimum consensus for renewing mandates of existing missions has always been reached so far. Russia and China have become increasingly critical about the related sanctions regimes and arms embargoes against the governments that host these peacekeeping missions. "As a result, there has arguably been a steady reduction in the political space for proactive, unified Security Council responses to new and emerging crises" (Duursma et al. 2023: 453). Moreover, the UN has also been blocked regarding recent major conflicts outside Africa, such as the wars in Syria, Ukraine and Gaza. In this context, three different scenarios for the future of multilateral peace operations can be distinguished.

5.1 SCENARIO 1: PRAGMATIC PEACE OPERATIONS UNDER UN UMBRELLA

Despite all dramatic geopolitical changes, the idea of multilateral peace operations could prove to be resilient, while materializing in a variety of pathways. In this scenario the UN would remain the normative and material centre of international peacekeeping, and continue to support a range of non-UN or UN-authorized peace operations with technical, financial, or logistical assistance. The UN would also retain unparalleled authority and legitimacy to convene key stakeholders when crises erupt. The Pact for the Future in September 2024 confirmed UN member state commitment for Peacebuilding but requested the Secretary-General to undertake a review of all forms of UN peace operations (UN 2024: Action 21).

In such a scenario, the UN might continue with some few larger multidimensional peace operations, but mostly concentrate on its mediation work through the provision of good offices and the deployment of SPMs, even in Syria or Yemen, where Special Envoy Offices have been established. An open question in this regard is, however, whether the past effectiveness of such civilian and diplomatic approaches has not been linked to the parallel employment of military force within peace operations.

Both the North Atlantic Treaty Organization and EU, as well as African organizations have proven their capacity to deploy larger peace operations. Should both the UN and regional organizations be involved in parallel missions in the same conflict theatre, cooperation could certainly be strengthened, either in a sequential logic (as has already happened between AU and UN) or in a more systematic division of tasks. This also emerges from the Independent Study on The Future of Peacekeeping commissioned by the UN in the wake of the Pact for the Future. The three experts propose a modular approach consisting of 30 different mission models, ranging from protection of civilians, and election security to cultural heritage protection and border management. Such a modular approach will allow future missions "to be tailored to unique situations, [...] and to adapt them over time and think through a wide range of partnerships, both inside and beyond the UN system" (Wane/Williams/Kihara-Hunt 2024: 5). From such a perspective, the diversity of actual peace operations is no longer regarded as an indicator for fragmentation and coordination challenges, but rather as a sign for pragmatism and for institutional innovation. At the same time, this strategy would also imply the clear recognition of many things UN peace operations cannot do in a given context.

The risk which comes with such a pragmatic approach to peace operations is that the UN might no longer be accepted as the legitimate orchestrator of global peace operations. So far, nearly all peace operations by organizations other than the UN have been authorized or at least recognized by the UN (Coleman/Williams 2021: 450). The strong urge to strengthen regionalization of peace operations, evident also in Guterres's New Agenda for Peace (UN 2023) – in which he offers support for building and rebuilding regional frameworks where there are not yet any – might also strengthen the idea of each region being responsible for its own peacekeeping, according to its own norms, and with a special expertise to deal with its own conflicts. This trend might also be observed in Europe with its new massive own security pressures.

5.2 SCENARIO 2: INCREASED UNILATERAL AND AD HOC INTERVENTIONISM

Even in the current context we already observe ad hoc coalitions not only going it alone, but also without the authorization of the UN Security Council. There is obviously a historical legacy of global powers acting without blessing of the UN Security Council, whether the US-led coalition in Iraq, or Russia in Georgia. The UN collective security system was never fully effective, with veto-members in the Security Council, the so-called "Permanent Five" (P5) protecting key allies from peace missions, or regional hegemons in Africa preventing African regional organizations from dealing with conflict situations on their territory.

While UN and UN-authorized peace missions were based on the key principle of impartiality and the idea to uphold some kind of collective security system, in this second scenario we see a growing number of such operations becoming more tailored to the achievement of specific political and military objectives, whether of intervening states or incumbent governments. Unilateral interventions and those based on "bilateral" agreements were the prerogative of global powers in the past (such as France's military interventionism in West Africa). We now observe countries such as Rwanda launching peace enforcement operations in other states with explicit host state consent (Central African Republic, Mozambique, Benin), but outside any mandate of African regional organizations. New international actors emerge, well-resourced mediators and dealmakers such as the Gulf Arab states, but their diplomatic activities seem hardly aligned to UN and AU mediation, and might include hidden unilateral military intervention. Informal "minilateral" coalitions and contact groups mobilize diplomatic resources which formalized international organizations lack, yet might also become forums for competition between actors with different ideas and interests regarding the conflict at hand (Whitfield 2025).

Russia's military invasion of Ukraine, but also China's and (more recently) the U.S.'s aggressive hegemonic claims, which are backed by open military posture, are a clear indicator of the return of coercive power (and credible military threats). While powerful states might be able to afford to go it alone, for many states (and their populations) in the Global South, this scenario is much less attractive. Rejection of multilateral peace operations might be a perfect populist move, but a global order without effective multilateral peacekeeping reduces the real exercise of sovereignty for many affected states and will increase the appetite of would-be hegemons.

5.3 SCENARIO 3: STRENGTHENING NON-MILITARY INTERVENTION PRACTICES

Since the 1990s UN peace operations were turning multidimensional not only insofar as they aimed at objectives larger than monitoring ceasefires, but also because they started to employ a wide range of instruments, military and non-military, to reach these objectives. UN thinking embedded peacekeeping within the broader concept of peacebuilding, including preventive and post-conflict instruments, such as early warning, or the facilitation of political dialogue after the cessation of violence (Abdenur 2019). Even where peace missions were operating amid violence, non-military practices were institutionalized, especially regarding mediation, protection of civilians and monitoring of human rights. The success of past UN multidimensional missions is attributed not only to the effective maintenance of security, but also to the missions' capacity to (re-)build rule of law, training of police forces, and securing a safe environment for humanitarian assistance (Wane/Williams/Kihara-Hunt 2024: 7).

In a third scenario, civilian aspects and political goals of peace missions are maintained and strengthened even in the absence of UN multidimensional operations. This could happen through two mechanisms. First, non-UN peace missions become more multidimensional by expanding their toolbox of non-military peacekeeping measures (Coleman/Williams 2021). Stockholm International Peace Research Institute (SIPRI) data on multilateral peace operations show that so far nearly all African peace operations are predominantly military missions, with some few police units, while nearly all current Organization for Security and Co-operation in Europe (OSCE) and EU missions are civilian (Pfeifer Cruz 2025: 14–15). The SIPRI focus on peace operations hides, however, the many non-military instruments that AU or ECOWAS have applied, most of which are employed independent of officially mandated peace operations (early warning, special envoys, mediation, electoral observation).[4] While more research is needed in understanding the many interfaces between military and non-military intervention practices, there is certainly a strong trajectory of civilian and political components of peace building (for example regarding anti-coup policies) which could be further developed and integrated (Witt/Hartmann/Engel 2025).

A second mechanism consists in a stronger integration of existing local, national, and UN-led peacebuilding structures into international intervention practices. Both the heavy international support for peacebuilding throughout the last four decades, and the local resistance against it, have strengthened local capacities and mobilized local, national and transnational networks of peace actors. Interestingly, Guterres's New Agenda for Peace also puts emphasis on "national infrastructures for peace" as the UN's key task in peacebuilding. This is a concept which has a long heritage in peace research and was introduced to the policy debates by the United Nations Development Programme (UNDP) in the early 2000s to promote multilayered peace networks which make best use of different local traditions, resources, and norms of peacebuilding (Odendaal 2021). In some countries it also triggered the formalization of institutional structures

4 A research network in which INEF is collaborating with the Peace Research Institute Frankfurt (PRIF) and University of Leipzig (African Non-Military Conflict Intervention Practices, ANCIP) is dedicated to making the many non-military interventions by African regional organizations more visible.

anchored within peace ministries or national peace councils. Guterres's approach mainly consists in appealing to governments and societal actors to jointly develop strategies about how to address domestic conflicts, rather than looking for international actors such as the UN to provide solutions. The UN's role would then consist in providing expertise and funding to national peace infrastructures, building on the work of the UN Peacebuilding Commission and Fund.

6. THE UNCLEAR FUTURE OF PEACE OPERATIONS

Many different factors will decide the fate of these scenarios, yet two aspects stand out as key variables. The future of peace operations critically depends on mobilizing *resources*. The UN also stopped mandating new large multidimensional peace operations because of budget constraints, and political missions have been supported within UN Security Council, because they are much less intrusive, but also much less expensive than sending troops (Karlsrud 2023: 226). African peace operations have been heavily financed by the EU and other Western actors. At the end of 2023, an agreement was reached about the UN financing up to 75% of future African peace operations. Non-military instruments have been, on the contrary, less costly [see Figure 6].

FIGURE 6: Expenditures for different UN peace activities
Comparison of budget development of different types of funding lines in USD (2014 compared to 2024)

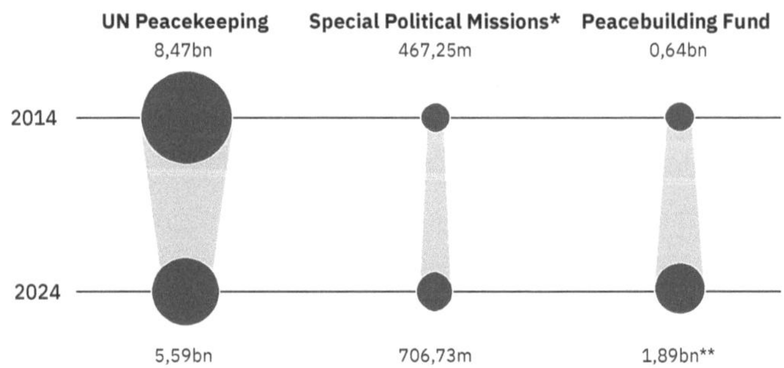

* **Proposed programme budget for the coming fiscal year; data includes:** Subject area I: Special representatives and personal envoys, advisers and representatives of the Secretary-General; Subject area III: Regional offices, offices supporting political processes and other missions; and UNAMA and UNAMI.
** As of November 2024

Source: Hansen et al. 2025: 13 (adapted version).

The mobilization of ad hoc coalitions further weakens the binding character of regional norms and standards, and is likely to reduce the willingness to further invest in collective security mechanisms and to maintain the idea that international peace is an international public good whose cost is also shared by the international community. Bilateral interventions (like those pursued by Rwanda) will rely on cash (or mineral resource) payment for security provision services delivered in other countries. Multilateral peace operations, on the contrary, have not been related to the availability of mineral resources in a conflict theatre.

A second critical variable concerns *shifting notions* of which understandings of peace future peace operations are supposed to promote. The original UN concern with maintaining international peace through pacifying interstate wars turned since the 1990s into the peace project of transforming divided societies through democratization and rule of law. As the liberal approach has lost much of its appeal, it has become unclear which peace doctrine guides peace missions. Looking at the three scenarios outlined here, most ad hoc missions are either counter-insurgency operations, or are promoting the stability of existing regimes, whose features might have contributed to the violent conflicts in the first place. A future of pragmatic peace operations under an UN umbrella might accommodate many different peace projects, but also de facto be restricted to more limited mandates or authorize stabilization missions. The very idea of peacebuilding, on the contrary, was built on the understanding that a sustainable peace requires building on resources and institutions which exist within conflict-affected societies, and that it necessarily needs to address root causes of conflicts and transforming conflictual relationships into cooperative ones.

The international community and policymakers from both the Global South and the Global North have thus many reasons to further support multilateral peace operations. Multidimensional missions might be further required, but should build on a coordinated division of roles between different actors and set political objectives which move beyond stabilizing incumbent regimes. Policymakers should also continue to advocate for a comprehensive approach to peacebuilding, which strategically integrates national and local infrastructures for peace into discussions about (continuation of) UN or non-UN peace operation mandates.

REFERENCES

Abdenur, Adriana Erthal 2019: Making Conflict Prevention a Concrete Reality at the UN (GLOBAL TRENDS.ANALYSIS 2/2019), Bonn.

Bastaki, Basil/Staniland, Paul/Popoola, Bryan 2024: Stabilizing Civil Wars Without Peacekeeping. Evidence from South Asia, in: International Security 49: 1, 133–170.

Boutros-Ghali, Boutros 1992: An Agenda for Peace. Preventive Diplomacy, Peacemaking and Peace-keeping. Report of the Secretary-General Pursuant to the Statement Adopted by the Summit Meeting of the Security Council on 31 January 1992 (UN Doc. S/24111), New York.

Coleman, Katharina P./Williams, Paul D. 2021: Peace Operations are What States Make of Them. Why Future Evolution is More Likely Than Extinction, in: Contemporary Security Policy 42: 2, 241–255.

Curran, David/Hunt, Charles T. 2020: Stabilization at the Expense of Peacebuilding in UN Peacekeeping Operations. More Than Just a Phase?, in: Global Governance 26: 1, 46–68.

Davies, Shawn/Pettersson, Therese/Sollenberg, Margareta/Öberg, Magnus 2025: Organized Violence 1989–2024, and the Challenges of Identifying Civilian Victims, in: Journal of Peace Research, 62: 4, 1223–1240.

de Coning, Cedric 2023: How Not to Do UN Peacekeeping. Avoid the Stabilization Dilemma with Principled and Adaptive Mandating and Leadership, in: Global Governance 29: 2, 152–167.

Duursma, Allard/Bara, Corinne/Wilén, Nina/Hellmüller, Sara/Karlsrud, John/Oksamytna, Kseniya/Bruker, Janek/Campell, Susanna/Cusimano, Salvator/Donati, Marco/Dorussen, Han/Druet, Dirk/Geier, Valentin/Epiney, Marine/Gelot, Linnéa/Gyllensporre, Dennis/Hiensch, Annick/Hultman, Lisa/Hunt, Charles T./Krishnan, Rajkumar Cheney/Labuda, Patryk I./Langenbach, Sascha/Hilding Norberg, Annika/Novosseloff, Alexandra/Oriesek, Daniel/Paddon Rhoads, Emily/Re, Francesco/Russo, Jenna/Sauter, Melanie/Smidt, Hannah/Staeger, Ueli/Wenger, Andreas 2023: UN Peacekeeping at 75. Achievements, Challenges, and Prospects, in: International Peacekeeping, 30: 4, 415–476.

Gowan, Richard/Forti, Daniel 2023: What Future for UN Peacekeeping in Africa After Mali Shutters Its Mission?, https://www.crisisgroup.org/global-mali/what-future-un-peacekeeping-africa-after-mali-shutters-its-mission; 08.09.2025.

Hansen, Annika S./Hansen, Wiebke/von Gienanth, Tobias/Benkler, Monika/Pietz, Tobias/Waehlisch, Martin 2025: UN-Friedenseinsätze. Fünf Trends und Fünf Chancen (Zentrum für Internationale Friedenseinsätze, Studie/Januar 2025), Berlin.

Hellmüller, Sara/Pinaud, Margaux/Lanfranchi, Chiara 2025: United Nations Peace Mission Mandates Dataset, Version 2.2, Geneva: Geneva Graduate Institute and Zürich: ETH Zürich, https://www.peacemissions.info/; 05.09.2025.

Karlsrud, John 2023: UN Peacekeeping Operations in a Multipolar Era, in: Global Governance 29: 2, 219–229.

Odendaal, Andries 2021: Local Infrastructures for Peace, in: Richmond, Oliver P./Visoka, Gëzim (eds.): The Oxford Handbook of Peacebuilding, Statebuilding, and Peace Formation, New York, 627–640.

Paris, Roland 2024: The Future of UN Peace Operations. Pragmatism, Pluralism or Statism?, in: International Affairs 100: 5, 2153–2172.

Pfeifer Cruz, Claudia 2025: Development and Trends in Multilateral Peace Operations, 2024 (SIPRI Fact Sheet May 2025), Stockholm.

United Nations (UN) 2000: Report of the Panel on United Nations Peace Operations (UN Doc. A/55/305), New York.

United Nations (UN) 2015a: Report of the High-Level Independent Panel on Peace Operations on Uniting our Strengths for Peace. Politics, Partnership and People (UN Doc. S/2015/446), New York.

United Nations (UN) 2015b: Partnering for Peace: Moving Towards Partnership Peacekeeping. Report of the Secretary-General (UN Doc. S/2015/229), New York.

United Nations (UN) 2023: A New Agenda for Peace. Our Common Agenda (Policy Brief), New York.

United Nations (UN) 2024: Pact for the Future. Global Digital Compact and Declaration on Future Generations (UN Doc. A/RES/79/1), New York.

Walter, Barbara F./Howard, Lise Morje/Fortna, V. Page 2021: The Extraordinary Relationship between Peacekeeping and Peace, in: British Journal of Political Science 51: 4, 1705–1722.

Wane, El-Ghassim/Williams, Paul D./Kihara-Hunt, Ai 2024: The Future of Peacekeeping, New Models, and Related Capabilities (Independent Study Commissioned by the UN Department of Peace Operations (DPO), October 2024), New York.

Whitfield, Teresa 2025: Minilateral Mechanisms for Peacemaking in a Multipolar World. Friends, Contact Groups, Troikas, Quads, and Quints (International Peace Institute, May 2025), New York.

Witt, Antonia/Hartmann, Christof/Engel, Ulf (eds.) 2026: African Non-military Conflict Intervention Practices, London.

Witt, Antonia/Hartmann, Christof/Engel, Ulf 2025: Studying African Non-Military Conflict Intervention Practices (ANCIP Working Papers 2/March 2025), Leipzig.

GLOBAL ECONOMY

CATCHING UP, PUSHING BACK: THE POLITICS OF DUE DILIGENCE IN GLOBAL VALUE CHAIN REGULATION

Christian Scheper and Markus Ciesielski

Abstract: This chapter analyses the global trend towards human rights and environmental due diligence in supply chain regulation, as well as the recent political backlash against it. Over the past two decades, regulation has shifted from voluntary soft law to binding hard law, with Europe at the forefront. National initiatives such as the French Duty of Vigilance and Germany's Supply Chain Act, together with the EU's Corporate Sustainability Due Diligence Directive, illustrate this long-term trend of "catching up" with a globalized economy through legal obligations. Yet this trajectory is increasingly contested: governments and business lobbies frame due diligence as a bureaucratic burden, while civil society critiques its limited effectiveness and corporate bias. Situating these dynamics in broader global political and economic developments, the chapter shows that due diligence regulation is not merely a technocratic adjustment but part of a larger trend of social struggle over corporate accountability, public authority, and the regulation of global production.

1. INTRODUCTION

Over the past fifteen years, governments have begun to rein in the global economy in a way that once seemed unlikely: by introducing binding obligations for companies to respect human rights and the environment across their global supply chains. France, Germany, and eventually the European Union (EU) took the lead, replacing voluntary guidelines with enforceable rules that reach far beyond national borders. The 2024 EU Corporate Sustainability Due Diligence Directive (CSDDD) marked a milestone in this shift. Yet, just as this trend gained momentum, it is now facing a countermovement. Political backlash and calls for deregulation raise the question of whether the era of "catching up" through supply chain legislation is already giving way to a new phase of pushback.

This pushback would mark a shift in the longer trend from *soft law*, such as non-binding guidelines or voluntary standards, to *hard law* – legally binding rules that companies must follow across borders. The trend towards hard law is remarkable for two reasons. Firstly, state regulation is largely entering uncharted transnational territory. Secondly, it appears to contradict broader developments in global politics, where powerful governments and economic actors have increasingly challenged and limited multilateral, rule-based trade policy.

These developments have accordingly triggered strong political controversy and recent pushbacks. In Germany, implementation of the national due diligence law, in force since 2023, faces increasing opposition within the government and in the parliament. The EU's move towards a harmonized CSDDD, after lengthy negotiations, could be significantly weakened compared to its initial ambition.[5] In the U.S., a broader political backlash against sustainability regulation has gained momentum. While criticism of supply chain legislation in the EU primarily draws on arguments of competitiveness, the need to reduce bureaucracy and to ease the burden on small and medium-sized enterprises, there is also scepticism from other sides: Criticism has also been voiced in academic circles and by human rights and environmental organizations. While they usually see these laws as important steps towards better human rights and environmental protection, they have criticized them as insufficient and too corporate-oriented, reproducing power imbalances rather than strengthening rights holders (Scheper 2025). The options for rights holders to lodge complaints and take legal action are often limited. Some also argue that supply chain governance needs to be "decolonized" – meaning it should better reflect the perspectives and interests of countries and communities that are often shaped by histories of colonial domination and economic dependency (Mason/Partzsch/Kramarz 2023).

The long-term trend of catching up with a globalized economy through supply chain legislation and the recent tendency to push it back raises the question of how we can interpret these developments. Where are we heading in terms of the regulation of global production? Drawing on political and legal developments of recent decades, the chapter identifies key trends and conflict lines and provides general policy recommendations.

5 At the time of writing, EU negotiations are still ongoing, but the positions of most governments indicate that the directive will be watered down.

The key point we emphasize is that the current policy of due diligence regulation does not mark the end of a debate or a mere technocratic adjustment but rather reflects a much broader social struggle over corporate responsibility, public authority and the regulation of the global economy. After a long evolution towards stronger legal regulation of global production, the new laws represent a long-fought compromise: while they introduce binding law on the regulation of human rights and the environment, their form is based on corporate supply chain management practices, i. e. risk-based, context-dependent duty of care rather than transnationally enforceable obligations to achieve specific results. The current countermovement against these laws is a new trend. It remains to be seen whether this is just a short phase or the beginning of a more fundamental reversal of an increasingly rights- and rule-based global production [see Figure 1]. In short: supply chain regulation remains a fundamentally contested field of the global political economy.

FIGURE 1: Trend of growing strength of binding regulations is slowing down
Transnational due diligence regulations since 2011

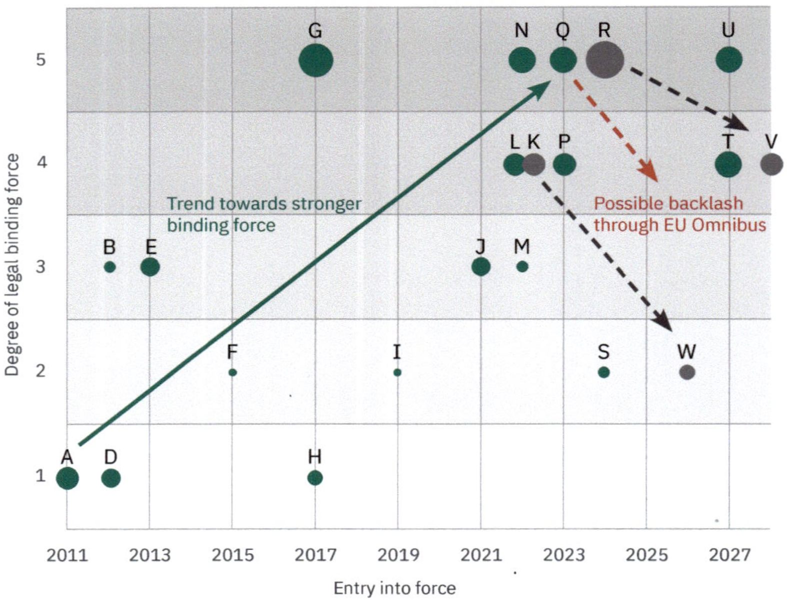

	Regulation	Entry into force
A	UN Guiding Principles	2011
B	USA Dodd-Frank §1502	2012
C	OECD Guidelines for MNEs (new human rights chapter)	2012
D	IFC Performance Standards	2012
E	EU Timber Regulation	2013
F	UK Modern Slavery Act	2015
G	France Loi de vigilance	2017
H	ILO MNE Declaration	2017
I	Australia Modern Slavery Act	2019
J	EU Conflict Minerals Regulation	2021
K	EU CSRD	2022
L	Norway Transparency Act	2022
M	Switzerland Due Diligence and Transparency Ordinance (VSoTr)	2022
N	USA UFLPA	2022
O	EUDR	2023
P	Germany LkSG	2023
Q	Mexican Forced Labour Import Ban	2023
R	EU CSDDD	2024
S	Canada S-211	2024
T	EU Battery Regulation	2027
U	EU Forced Labour Regulation	2027
V	EU CSDDD (Omnibus proposal)	2028
W	EU CSRD (Omnibus proposal)	2026

Circle size: The size corresponds with our rating of the regulatory impact, which we interpret based on four criteria: scope, rights covered, administrative enforceability and civil liability. Each was rated from 1 (weak) to 3 (strong).
Degrees of legal binding force: We differentiate five levels: Level 1: No binding nature/soft law; Level 2: Primarily reporting and transparency obligations; Level 3: Thematically limited due diligence obligations; Level 4: Holistic due diligence obligations with regulatory enforcement; Level 5: Holistic due diligence obligations with civil law recourse.

Source: Own compilation.

2. EARLY BEGINNINGS OF CATCHING UP: GLOBAL VALUE CHAINS AND THE ONGOING STRUGGLE FOR REGULATION

Since the 1970s, the rise of outsourcing (shifting production steps to external companies) and offshoring (relocating production to other countries) has transformed integrated firms into globally dispersed value chains, reinforcing asymmetrical power relations between lead firms in the Global North and suppliers in the Global South. While this restructuring enabled unprecedented global integration and economic growth, it entrenched structural inequalities and generated severe risks for labour rights, human rights, and the environment.

A brief guide through the supply chain terminology

The term "supply chain", which people often use in everyday business and legal discourse, originated in the field of business administration. It focuses on the flow of goods and compliance rules from the perspective of management. This business perspective also shapes everyday language and most legal discussions. In the wider social sciences, by contrast, researchers more commonly use the term "global value chains" (GVCs).

As described by Ponte/Gereffi/Raj-Reichert (2019: 1), a GVC encompasses "the full range of activities that firms, farmers and workers carry out to bring a product or service from its conception to its end use, recycling or reuse. These activities include design, production, processing, assembly, distribution, maintenance and repair, disposal/recycling, marketing, finance and consumer services".

The GVC perspective then, which we take in the remainder of this chapter, looks at the full range of activities that create and capture value – from raw materials to finished products.

Some researchers also prefer the term "global production networks", emphasizing the wider social context of production, such as state institutions and labour geographies. The term "global commodity chains", finally, emphasizes material flows and exchange relationships, usually from a world-systems perspective, highlighting hierarchical relations between core and periphery (Gibbon et al. 2008).

From time to time, different combinations of the terms are also used. While each term stands for a specific research tradition and perspective, these perspectives often speak to each other and overlap.

2.1 FROM SOFT LAW TO HARD LAW: REGULATORY EVOLUTION 1970–2010

Efforts to regulate the social and environmental consequences of GVCs through binding international norms have a long and contested history. Over the last fifty years, we can see repeated attempts to bring transnational economic activities back under social control, i.e. to set rules that make global business more accountable to societies and communities (Langthaler/Schüssler 2019). In the 1970s, the United Nations Commission on Transnational Corporations (UNCTC) already attempted to establish a code of conduct for transnational corporations (TNCs), but diverging, influential economic interests blocked its adoption. The 1980s saw the rise of the neoliberal economic paradigm, which holds that the market forces of supply and demand are the best way to coordinate societies. State control and forms of common ownership were increasingly viewed as problematic. As a result, privatization, corporate self-regulation, and – in many parts of the world – the active suppression of trade unions became dominant tools of economic governance.

In the 1990s, the prevailing regulatory policy shifted away from the radical belief in free markets, but transnational regulation remained predominantly private. Regimes of private transnational governance became a prevalent paradigm, which adhered to private-sector solutions to social and ecological challenges. They aimed at promoting human rights and sustainability along GVCs based on the private profit interests of large lead firms but still lacked obligatory enforcement mechanisms and state-driven monitoring.

In the late 1990s, new attempts were made to hold corporations accountable, this time with a focus on international human rights law. The United Nations "Norms on the Responsibilities of Transnational Corporations and Other Business Enterprises with regard to Human Rights" from 2003 (or short: UN Norms) were proposed as a binding international obligation for TNCs. However, they failed to gain political traction and were only adopted as a framework without legal effect (Weissbrodt/Kruger 2003). Against this backdrop, John Ruggie was appointed as the UN Secretary-General's Special Representative for Business and Human Rights. He had already co-designed the UN Global Compact, a voluntary UN initiative promoting corporate commitment to human rights and sustainability that had been established in 2000. Ruggie introduced the concept of "principled pragmatism", drawing on New Governance Theory, an approach that emphasizes flexible, participatory, and pragmatic regulation over rigid legal mandates (Backer 2017). His approach emphasized three elements: the state duty to protect human rights through public policies, the corporate responsibility to respect human rights, and the importance of access to effective complaint mechanisms and legal remedies. In doing so, he remained committed to soft law throughout his mandates, but by emphasizing the importance of legal remedies, he laid an important foundation for subsequent political debates: Functioning legal mechanisms were emphasized as essential if rights holders were to be able to make claims and address grievances.

In 2011, after extensive consultations, the UN Human Rights Council unanimously supported Ruggie's approach and endorsed the UN Guiding Principles on Business and Human Rights (UNGPs) (Backer 2017). These principles marked a milestone in the evolution of GVC regulation, providing a soft law framework that structured corporate due diligence as a key mechanism to prevent human rights violations and environmental harm. It emphasizes the role of the state, as well as the importance of transnational corporations and their self-interest as levers for international norms and rule enforcement. While the approach does not exclude binding legal regulation, the binding nature of laws was less important in the framework than the pragmatic consideration of building international consensus. Nevertheless, the approach demonstrated significant potential for further civil society activism and political discourse surrounding the selective enforcement of legally binding instruments in the years following the adoption of the UNGPs.

2.2 THE RISE OF MANDATORY DUE DILIGENCE SINCE 2010

Following the 2008/09 financial crisis, governments increasingly adopted public rules to make companies more transparent about supply-chain risks. Section 1502 of the U.S. Dodd-Frank Act (2010) requires reporting on the use of "conflict minerals" from the Democratic Republic of the Congo and neighbouring countries, while the UK Modern Slavery Act (2015) and Australia's Modern Slavery Act (2018) require large companies to publish annual statements on steps taken against forced labour. These measures centre on transparency and let authorities act if firms fail to report, but they stop short of a broad legal duty to prevent abuses across the whole supply chain. The EU Timber Regulation (2013) goes a step further: it bans illegally harvested timber from the EU market and requires companies to conduct due-diligence checks in an issue-specific way. The French

Duty of Vigilance Law (Loi de Vigilance) of 2017 represented another landmark in hard law regulation. It was the first law that – in a more holistic fashion – required large companies to implement and publish vigilance plans covering human rights and environmental risks in their supply chains. Germany's Supply Chain Due Diligence Act (LkSG, Lieferkettensorgfaltspflichtengesetz), effective from January 2023, followed a similar logic, with a more limited scope but with relatively extensive official powers of enforcement. Although the law excludes civil liability, it allows complaints from civil society to be lodged with the relevant public authority: the Federal Office for Economic Affairs and Export Control (BAFA, Bundesamt für Wirtschaft und Ausfuhrkontrolle). The Transparency Act in Norway, in force since 2022, similarly requires due diligence steps by companies with effective sanctioning.

Some countries have also introduced issue-specific laws, that either demand due diligence processes, such as the Dutch Child Labour Law[1], or ban products that are produced under violation of fundamental rights, such as the Uyghur Forced Labor Prevention Act in the U.S. (2022) and the Forced Labor Ban in Mexico (2023).

Overall, it is clear that an increasingly complex landscape of different due diligence laws is emerging. While transparency was initially the main focus, this has gradually been supplemented by issue-specific import restrictions and more holistic due diligence obligations. The trend towards hard law can therefore be viewed in more detail, as the nature of the legislation is also changing. This development can be observed particularly at EU level, which is likely to continue contributing to the harmonization of its member states' regulations in the coming years.

2.3 EUROPE'S PIONEERING ROLE IN GVC REGULATION

The EU's CSDDD was originally proposed in 2020 by then-Justice Commissioner Didier Reynders. It aimed to create a harmonized framework even surpassing national laws like the German LkSG by including civil liability and covering a wider range of companies. This was heavily contested by various governments and interest groups. The CSDDD was formally adopted in 2024 in a much less

1 The law was adopted by the Dutch Senate in 2019, but its enforcement is still pending.

ambitious form. It establishes phased, binding human rights and environmental due diligence duties for large EU and non-EU companies, but its exact scope and reach is still up for debate at the time of writing.

The EU Taxonomy for sustainable activities introduced a common classification system for environmentally sustainable economic activities. Entering into force in 2020, it is intended to help investors and companies by providing a shared definition of what constitutes sustainability, creating investor confidence, preventing "greenwashing", and directing capital towards sustainable activities. In parallel, the Corporate Sustainability Reporting Directive (CSRD) (2023) mandates harmonized sustainability disclosures using the European Sustainability Reporting Standards (ESRS) adopted on 31 July 2023, thereby reinforcing transparency and comparability. The EU Deforestation Regulation (EUDR) targets forest-risk commodities with traceability and due diligence requirements. It has also been highly contested. Following a 12-month phase-in period, obligations will apply to large and medium-sized operators from the end of 2025 and to small companies from mid-2026. Together, CSDDD, CSRD/ESRS, and the Taxonomy form the core of an increasingly comprehensive, yet institutionally fragmented, EU sustainability governance regime for GVCs.

This core is flanked by a broader set of EU instruments, such as the EUDR, that shape incentives, market access and organizational practice, including: a forced-labour market ban, sector-/product-specific due diligence, circularity-driven product rules and digital product passports, climate-trade measures, sustainable-finance transparency, consumer protection against greenwashing, and agri-food power asymmetry rules.

A detailed examination of the underlying regulations would go beyond the scope of this chapter, but Figure 2 shows that an increasingly complex ecosystem of regulations is emerging, underscoring the normative trend toward growing social and environmental due diligence obligations for transnational companies in the EU.

FIGURE 2: An increasingly dense landscape of GVC sustainability regulation in the EU

Core due diligence obligations and flanking regulations

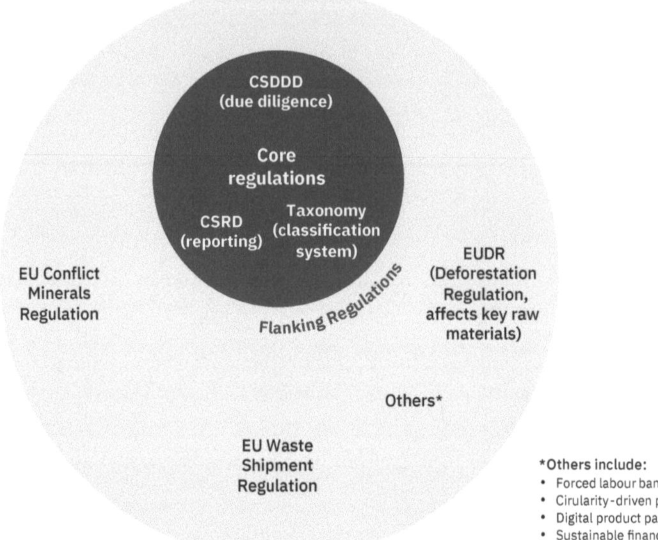

Source: Own compilation.

The effects of the new due diligence obligations are still difficult to assess. This is not only because they are new, but also because they are ambivalent in nature. On the one hand, they introduce new rules for companies. On the other hand, they grant extensive powers to management and private intermediaries for their implementation (Scheper 2025). This has also proven problematic with soft law solutions, as governance fails precisely when conflicts of interest arise for the company. Furthermore, beyond formal due diligence rules, compliance outcomes are influenced by purchasing practices. Pricing, lead times, order variability and the allocation of contractual risk can all contribute to the externalization of business risks and compliance costs, thereby undermining the supplier's remediation capacity. Including buying practices in the scope of due diligence regulation shifts the focus of compliance from supplier audits to a shared responsibility challenge throughout the supply chain. However, this has not been a focus of existing regulations to date, and it seems increasingly sidelined as pushbacks against new regulation intensify.

3. BACKLASH TENDENCY AND ONGOING REGULATORY STRUGGLE

After decades in which human rights and environmental regulation of GVCs was contested but ultimately pushed forward step by step, there has been significant headwind in recent years, and it is unclear whether the regulatory efforts will take a new path. In view of the perceived polycrisis of the global economy and a rise of governments that criticize international legal rules, the regulation of human rights and environmental standards is being portrayed by influential actors as an unacceptable bureaucratic hurdle and a geopolitical misstep. We can clearly see this pressure on due diligence regulation on the EU level: Following its adoption, the CSDDD has faced significant opposition. In response, civil society actors, trade unions and Nongovernmental Organizations (NGOs) defend the relevance and progress of due diligence laws. New publications that reiterate the arguments in favour of due diligence regulations demonstrate the ongoing political struggle for regulation (Saage-Maaß/Korn 2025).

3.1 THE GERMAN LKSG LIMBO AND THE EU CSDDD: STEAMROLLED BY THE OMNIBUS?

In Germany, the implementation of the LkSG has faced increasing opposition from the beginning. At the time of writing, we can witness a de facto moratorium on enforcement, the implications of which are unclear. In light of the crises widely perceived to be facing the German economy, especially since 2022 (including the consequences of the pandemic and energy shortages resulting from Russia's war against Ukraine), German governments have resisted implementing the LkSG consistently. Criticism focuses on "bureaucratic burdens" and potential competitive disadvantages for German firms. The federal government's stance led to a dormant regulatory status of the law, in which the LkSG continues to exist and, in view of the adopted CSDDD, cannot simply be repealed under European law, but at the same time companies are no longer sanctioned if they fail to fulfil their due diligence obligations (as of August 2025).

At the EU level, the initially ambitious CSDDD has also been substantially weakened after prolonged negotiations. The backlash has recently materialized in the "Omnibus I package", proposed in February 2025 by the European Commission. The simplification bundle aims at reducing administrative burdens on businesses and enhancing competitiveness. The Omnibus would streamline sustainability reporting under CSRD and the EU Taxonomy, and temper due diligence obligations under the CSDDD. Subsequently, in June 2025, the EU Council adopted its position, endorsing measures to roll back some Environmental, Social, and Governance-related (ESG) requirements in the interests of greater market efficiency. This reflects a significant shift: while the CSDDD still stands, its enforcement mechanisms and compliance thresholds have been softened in response to concerns raised by member states and powerful industry interests. In addition to restrictions on content, the most important aspects here are the limitation of the scope of application to significantly fewer companies and the deletion of harmonized civil liability rules. The omnibus proposal is still subject to approval by the Council and Parliament, so at this point we are only presenting the voting positions of influential member states that have taken a clear stance [see Figure 3].

FIGURE 3: Initially ambitious CSDDD could be substantially weakened

Positions taken by the largest four economies of the EU on CSDDD in Omnibus negotiations 2025

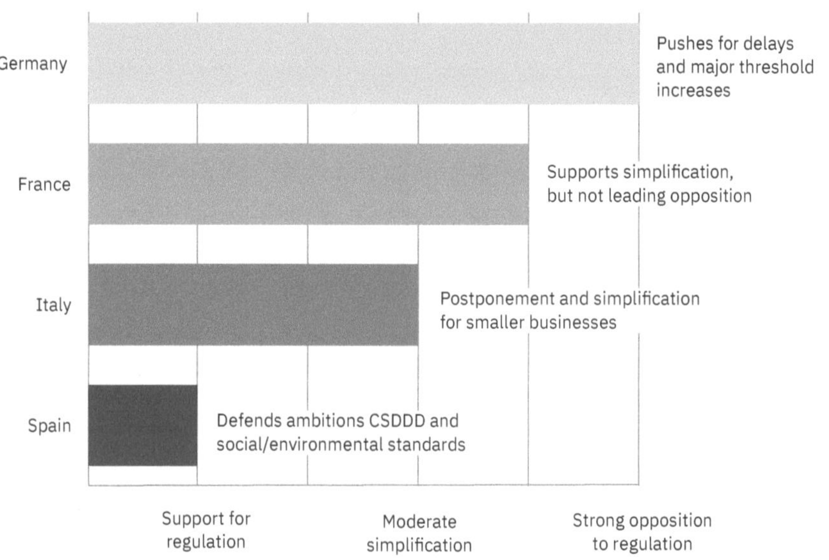

Note: The classification only covers the largest four economies in the EU and is based on a qualitative interpretation of their publicly reported positions during the EU Council negotiations on the Omnibus I package in early to mid-2025.

Source: Own compilation based on public reporting on country positions in early to mid-2025, see https://www.reuters.com/sustainability/eu-countries-split-over-whether-delay-green-reporting-rules-2025-02-19/; 31.08.2025.

3.2 PUTTING THE RECENT BACKLASH INTO A WIDER POLITICAL CONTEXT

The recent backlash against GVC regulation cannot be fully understood without situating it within broader global political and economic developments. Across many regions, including the EU, the U.S., India, and Latin America (especially Argentina), political landscapes have shifted towards increasingly libertarian-authoritarian, or otherwise anti-democratic orientations (International Research Group on Authoritarianism and Counter-Strategies 2022). These trends have implications for regulatory approaches to corporate accountability and sustainability governance.

At the same time, GVCs have acquired a central role in geopolitics. Their significance is not only reflected in the sheer volume of global trade organized through GVCs but also in their growing presence within legal frameworks and the intense contestation surrounding regulatory efforts. The geopolitical salience of GVCs became particularly evident during the COVID-19 pandemic, when supply chain disruptions and heightened awareness of critical dependencies prompted intense public and political debate. The war in Ukraine further underscored these dynamics, as disruptions in wheat trade and other critical raw materials from Russia and Ukraine highlighted vulnerabilities in global production and logistics networks. New trade routes and initiatives such as China's Belt and Road Initiative have become focal points of competition and regulatory concern in international relations (cf. Müller 2025).

In this context, the U.S. also plays a pivotal role. While protectionist and nationalist trade policies gained prominence under the Trump administration, the retreat from multilateral trade governance had already begun during the Obama years, notably through the U.S.'s obstruction of the World Trade Organization's dispute resolution mechanism that still paralyzes the organization. In recent years, however, this trend has massively shifted towards concerted political campaigns and government actions against private sector ESG standards and investments. The "anti-ESG movement" driven by the U.S. government has included high-profile measures such as the freezing of climate funds, lawsuits against regulatory agencies, and the repeal of Biden-era fiduciary rules on ESG considerations in investment decisions. For example, the U.S. Department of Labor officially dropped ESG-related fiduciary guidance for retirement plans, fundamentally reshaping the regulatory landscape for sustainable finance (Johnson 2025). Lawsuits such as Climate United v. E. P. A. (Environmental Protection Agency) further illustrate the intensified contestation of environmental governance at the federal level. Even if the current administration changes, the anti-ESG momentum may have lasting repercussions. It could reduce the availability of capital for supply chain sustainability initiatives and weaken the financial incentives that underpin compliance with due diligence laws, thereby reducing the effectiveness of regulation well beyond the current political cycle [see Figure 4] (Bioy 2025).

FIGURE 4: Consolidation of ESG investment after a backlash?

Inflows and outflows in global sustainability funds, in billions of USD (Q2/2022 – Q2/2025)

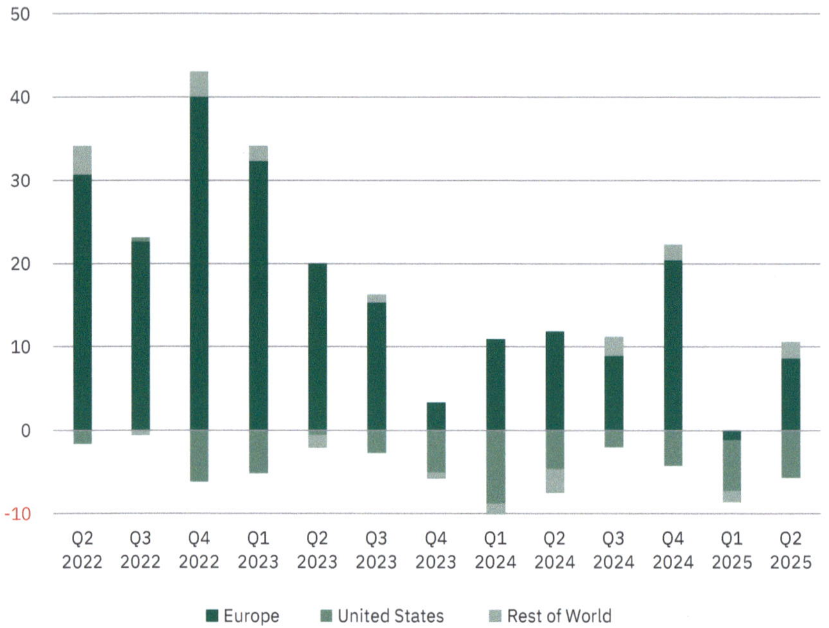

Note: Sustainability funds here include open-ended and exchange-traded funds that focus on sustainability and ESG factors or impact.

Source: Bioy 2025 (data as of June 2025; adapted version).

4. GLOBAL SPILLOVER EFFECTS AND STRATEGIC ADAPTATION IN GVCS

The regulatory challenges surrounding due diligence and corporate sustainability in Europe could have wide-reaching and even unintended consequences for the global economy. Some major suppliers to Europe, such as those in Bangladesh, Vietnam and Brazil, are under increased pressure to comply with new regulations from their customers, often without adequate support for capacity building or facilitating market access. There is also a risk that leading companies will outsource their obligations to suppliers without reviewing and reforming their own purchasing practices and GVC strategies with regard to risk. Some companies change suppliers to fulfil their due diligence obligations more easily, for example by using certified raw materials, purchasing from larger suppliers with better risk management systems or greater transparency, or bundling their purchases from suppliers over whom they have greater influence. Some suppliers and export-oriented countries may therefore view the regulatory changes as a threat to their profits. Others, however, see them as a competitive opportunity and are increasing production capacity in line with international sustainability standards.

To date, there is a lack of empirical knowledge about the global spillover effects of legal due diligence requirements. We can, however, assume that several structural factors amplify the transnational consequences of regulatory shifts. Firstly, the global character of production with its unequal global distribution of buying power but also of critical raw materials, such as rare earths or agri-food, means that regulatory changes in major markets such as the EU and the U.S. have repercussions worldwide. Resources such as cobalt from the Democratic Republic of the Congo, and palm oil from Indonesia and Malaysia, are essential to numerous global production processes (Pelon et al. 2021). Any new due diligence or traceability requirements imposed by large economies impact market conditions and regulatory responses in supplier countries.

Secondly, the highly financialized character of the global economy can act as a significant amplifier or brake on regulatory change. Large institutional investors, asset managers and rating agencies incorporate ESG factors into their risk assessments and investment decisions. This creates cross-border pressure on companies and governments, even in countries without formal due diligence requirements, as access to global capital increasingly depends on sustainability credentials. At the same time, the anti-ESG pressure that we are currently seeing in the U. S. will have a global impact. The consequences for Europe and other parts of the world are not yet clear. It could either exert additional pressure or drive ESG investments to other parts, especially to Europe. These investments remain hugely important, as due diligence requirements alone cannot bring about change – they only regulate management processes, not human rights or environmental *outcomes*. Change in GVCs eventually depends on changing corporate strategies. In turn, the strategies of large companies and small and medium-sized enterprises alike will depend on financial investment decisions (Ferretti 2023).

Thirdly, accelerated digitalization is changing the way regulatory requirements are disseminated and enforced. Indeed, the GVC perspective on issues of structure, agency, and governance must be reviewed considering an increasing relevance of platform economies and Artificial Intelligence (AI) developments (Butollo et al. 2022, Foster/Graham 2017). Increasingly, strategies for implementing private governance measures along the GVC seem to be determined by questions of data manageability. While platforms, digital data management for certification, and supply chain management can greatly increase the speed and reach of governance, the types of data collection may not adequately represent real-world production conditions and their impact on humans and the environment. The genuinely political nature of GVC governance then might become increasingly invisible and appear to be merely a technical challenge. AI technologies and their integration into all areas of life raise new questions about human work behind the supposedly purely automatic AI machinery (Muldoon/Graham/Cant 2024). This is likely to cause ongoing problems for workers and trade unions trying to collectively defend their rights.

Fourthly, in the wake of ESG and due diligence regulations, transnational legal mobilization is also intensifying. For example, there have been border-crossing lawsuits in cases of industrial catastrophes in Brazil's mining sector, which is a bottleneck of the steel industry in the Global North. Interestingly, the German LkSG was not in effect when legal proceedings began. However, local claimants and international NGOs refer to due diligence in the course of the still-pending processes (Mentrup 2024). If references to ESG regulations and due diligence norms prove to be part of a broader trend, then we could speak of a shift towards due diligence legal consciousness. This shift could alter the role of NGOs and civil society by influencing how non-governmental actors approach global corporate accountability in the future. Thus, it will contribute to the legal transformation of how GVCs are interpreted, which is indispensable for further legal mobilization. This could create future opportunities to strengthen related transnational production agendas, such as those of trade unions.

Strategic adaptation by key supplier countries is already underway. China, in particular, plays a dual role as both a regulatory shaper and a competitor. While selectively aligning with Western sustainability standards, China actively promotes its own GVC structures and regulatory frameworks through initiatives such as the Belt and Road Initiative, the Digital Silk Road, and domestic ESG standards tailored to national priorities. Regional regulatory cooperation mechanisms, such as the Association of Southeast Asian Nations (ASEAN), also reflect efforts to establish alternative sustainability frameworks outside the dominant EU and U.S. models. Competing norms require a comprehensive understanding. It should be noted that effective regulation of GVCs is only one consequence of due diligence norms. Even outdated norms may still create a consciousness able to mobilize interest groups in trade unions, civil society and NGOs. In this sense, the effects of GVC norms extend beyond the scope of regulations, obligations, and enforcement structures.

5. FUTURE PATHS: A CRITICAL TURNING POINT FOR GVC REGULATION?

As this chapter has shown, a years-long trend towards more comprehensive GVC regulation has recently given way to a backlash. The future of human rights and sustainability policies in GVCs is uncertain.

Against this backdrop, it is important to highlight some key requirements of GVC regulation that take underlying political conflicts into account. Poverty wages, high health and environmental risks of production, and problems with education and social security for workers persist when GVC norms are not implemented or dismissed. Ambivalent experiences with soft law demonstrate that regulation should enable employees' and other rights holders to assert their own claims, organize themselves and take legal action, even against the interests of powerful companies or governments in cases of conflict. This is central to making transnational regulations effective. As long as companies are more or less solely responsible for implementation along GVCs, today's human rights and environmental problems along GVCs will not be solved. Given the uncertain future in the current backlash, one undeniable fact remains: regulations may be repealed, but conflicts persist. We should under no circumstances assume that the automatic response will be lengthy projects returning to GVC legislation. However, we should expect civil society protests, new regulatory demands, strikes and transnational legal actions, as well as people in the Global South who feel they have been treated unfairly. The current backlash may affect grievance instruments and regulations. Nevertheless, those in power should be aware that this will pave the way for civil societies and electorates who are outraged by the unequal distribution of risks and gains around the world.

6. POLICY RECOMMENDATIONS TO EU DECISION MAKERS AND NATIONAL REGULATION AUTHORITIES

Over the past two decades, regulation has shifted from voluntary soft law to binding hard law, with Europe at the forefront. Yet this chapter has shown how this trajectory is increasingly contested: governments and business lobbies frame due diligence as a bureaucratic burden, while civil society critiques its limited effectiveness and corporate bias. The following recommendations outline how existing regulations can be further developed and more effectively implemented in the interest of rights holders. They highlight key levers such as accessible remedies for rights holders, stronger public institutions, coherent implementation of core regulatory frameworks, responsible purchasing practices, the use of digital tools for transnational enforcement, and meaningful stakeholder participation. Together, these measures help close protection gaps, strengthen the enforceability of rights, and ensure regulation remains aligned with the overarching objectives of human rights due diligence.

- **Put rights holders at the centre to enable effective remedy:**
  Establish accessible administrative complaint mechanisms (clear timelines, anti-retaliation safeguards, local languages) and expand civil liability, including options for collective redress. Protect human rights defenders and pilot worker-led processes and monitoring in GVCs.

- **Strengthen the role of public institutions to support rights holders:**
  Establish, maintain and develop public institutions such as public defenders, ombuds institutions and legal aid services that support rights holders in using

available complaint mechanisms and legal remedies for effective assistance. Pay particular attention to gender equality and sensitivity to minorities, including persons with disabilities.

- **Consolidate the rule-based core of regulation by putting substance over form:** Implement CSDDD, CSRD/ESRS, EUDR and flanking regulations coherently, without dilution and overwhelming red tape, i. e. resource supervisory authorities, provide clear guidance, and apply proportionality without hollowing out material due diligence duties.
- **Focus on purchasing practices to introduce shared responsibility in buyer-driven GVCs:**
  Mandate responsible purchasing (prices, lead times, order variability, supplier onboarding and disengagement) and link compliance expectations to buying behaviour. Strengthen enforcement of trading rules and leverage public procurement to reward credible due diligence.
- **Use digital tools to build transnational enforcement capacity, but not "data-only":**
  Support cross-border cooperation and joint investigations; co-invest with producing countries in supplier upgrading and audit alternatives. Use open, interoperable data standards (e. g., product passports) with privacy protections, and track outcome metrics (e. g., living wages, zero deforestation) alongside Key Performance Indicators. Support worker-driven digital platforms and initiatives.
- **Deepen institutional pathways for better participation by applying gender, intersectionality and vulnerability lenses to regulation:**
  Define meaningful stakeholder engagement with minimum standards (including unions and communities). Require gender-responsive due diligence and explicit consideration of migrants and informal workers; embed stakeholders in grievance handling and follow-up to ensure remedies are implemented.

REFERENCES

Backer, Larry Catá 2017: Principled Pragmatism in the Elaboration of a Comprehensive Treaty on Business and Human Rights, in: Deva, Surya/Bilchitz, David (eds.): Building a Treaty on Business and Human Rights. Context and Contours, Cambridge, 105–130.

Bioy, Hortense 2025: Global ESG Fund Flows Rebound in Q2 2025 Despite ESG Backlash and Geopolitical Uncertainty (25.07.2025), https://www.morningstar.com/sustainable-investing/global-esg-fund-flows-rebound-q2-2025-despite-esg-backlash-geopolitical-uncertainty; 31.08.2025.

Butollo, Florian/Gereffi, Gary/Yang, Chun/Krzywdzinski, Martin 2022: Digital Transformation and Value Chains. Introduction, in: Global Networks 22: 4, 585–594.

Ferretti, Tommaso 2023: Impact Investing and Sustainable Global Value Chains. Enabling Small and Medium Enterprises Sustainability Strategies, in: AIB Insights 23: 5. DOI: 10.46697/001c.88529.

Foster, Christopher/Graham, Mark 2017: Reconsidering the Role of the Digital in Global Production Networks, in: Global Networks 17: 1, 68–88.

Gibbon, Peter/Bair, Jennifer/Ponte, Stefano 2008: Governing Global Value Chains. An Introduction, in: Economy and Society 37: 3, 315–338.

International Research Group on Authoritarianism and Counter-Strategies (ed.) 2022: Global Authoritarianism, Bielefeld.

Johnson, Lamar 2025: Labor Dept. Drops Biden-era ESG Fiduciary Rule, https://www.esgdive.com/news/labor-dept-drops-biden-era-esg-fiduciary-401k-rule-will-remake-regulation/749312/; 01.09.2025.

Langthaler, Ernst/Schüßler, Elke 2019: Commodity Studies with Polanyi. Disembedding and Re-Embedding Labour and Land in Contemporary Capitalism, in: Österreichische Zeitschrift für Soziologie 44: 2, 209–223.

Mason, Michael/Partzsch, Lena/Kramarz, Teresa 2023: The Devil is in the Detail—The Need for a Decolonizing Turn and Better Environmental Accountability in Global Supply Chain Regulations. A Comment, in: Regulation & Governance 17: 4, 970–979.

Mentrup, Theresa 2024: Die Katastrophe von Brumadinho und die deutsche Verantwortung, in: Blätter für deutsche und internationale Politik 24: 1, 29–33.

Muldoon, James/Graham, Mark/Cant, Callum 2024: Feeding the Machine. The Hidden Human Labour Powering AI, Edinburgh.

Müller, Melanie 2025: Die Geopolitik globaler Lieferketten (Schriftenreihe Band 10998, Bundeszentrale für politische Bildung), Bonn.

Pelon, Remi/Hund, Kirsten Lori/Fabregas Masllovet, Thao Phuong/De Sa, Paulo/Mcmahon, Gary Joseph Raymond 2021: Cobalt in the Democratic Republic of Congo. Market Analysis (English) (Report No. 168468, World Bank Group), Washington, D.C.

Ponte, Stefano/Gereffi, Gary/Raj-Reichert, Gale 2019: Introduction to the Handbook on Global Value Chains, in: Ponte, Stefano/Gereffi, Gary/Raj-Reichert, Gale (eds.): Handbook on Global Value Chains, Cheltenham, 1–27.

Saage-Maaß, Miriam/Korn, Franziska 2025: Lieferkettengesetze. Menschenrechte für eine nachhaltige Wirtschaft. Ein Argumentationsleitfaden (Friedrich-Ebert-Stiftung e.V.), Bonn.

Scheper, Christian 2025: Corporate Due Diligence in Global Value Chains, in: Moore, Madelaine/Scherrer, Christoph/van der Linden, Marcel (eds.): The Elgar Companion to Decent Work and the Sustainable Development Goals, Cheltenham, 370–381.

Weissbrodt, David S./Kruger, Muria 2003: Norms on the Responsibilities of Transnational Corporations and Other Business Enterprises with Regard to Human Rights, in: American Journal of International Law 97: 4, 901–922.

ENVIRONMENT AND NATURAL RESOURCES

BRIDGING DIVIDES: WATER DIPLOMACY AS A TOOL FOR CONFLICT TRANSFORMATION

Marcus Kaplan

Abstract: Although water is of vital importance for livelihoods and for economic and social development, roughly one quarter of mankind still lacks access to safe water services. Global water resources are under severe stress due to increasing demands and reduced availability and quality. In combination with social, political, and economic factors, water stress may trigger intra- and interstate conflicts. Water diplomacy is a promising concept for addressing the linkages between water and conflict, as it takes an inclusive and cooperative approach, aiming to not only contribute to water-related issues, but rather focussing on wider goals related to stability, peace, development, and equity. Water diplomacy thus has the potential of counteracting the current global trends towards unilateralism, securitization, and water weaponization. This chapter analyses the benefits of water diplomacy, but also some of the challenges, which hamper its effective implementation. It also explores the interrelations between water diplomacy and the fragmented architecture of global water governance, which thus far remains insufficiently equipped to manage the mounting pressures on freshwater resources and the associated potential for conflict.

1. INTRODUCTION

Water is a basis for livelihoods and for economic activities around the world: people need access to safe drinking water for survival, agriculture is the largest user of freshwater globally[1], and many industries such as energy, mining, and construction rely heavily on water. In 2010, the United Nations (UN) General Assembly declared access to safe and clean drinking water and sanitation a human right, and it called on states and international organizations to provide resources, tech-

1 See https://www.science.org/content/article/agriculture-sucking-fresh-water-dry; 26.09.2025.

nology, and capacity building to help ensure universal access. This was taken up again 2015 in the 2030 Agenda for Sustainable Development, where Sustainable Development Goal (SDG) 6 calls for "ensuring availability and sustainable management of water and sanitation for all". In addition, water is also fundamental for achieving many of the other SDGs. Although the number of people with access to safe drinking water has risen steadily in recent decades, 2.1 billion people – roughly one in four people worldwide – still lacked safely managed drinking water services in 2024.[2] Progress on SDG 6 is thus still significantly off-track.[3]

Global freshwater resources are under severe stress due to various factors: Demand for water is increasing, while availability and quality is shrinking. Population growth and rising living standards result in more people requiring access to larger quantities of water and food, industrialization and energy production also increase water consumption, and pollution through agricultural or industrial activities leaves water sources unsafe for human use or even completely unusable. Furthermore, many regions around the world already suffer from the impacts of climate change: flooding events occur more often, rainfall becomes unreliable, glaciers, which are important sources of freshwater, melt and, due to rising temperatures, evaporation increases. Shifts in water availability can put pressure on people's livelihoods, as they may need to spend more time collecting water or face higher costs to purchase safe drinking water. It affects food security and may also cause a higher prevalence of waterborne diseases. Furthermore, it may lead to aquifer depletion and reductions in the provision of ecosystem services. The topic also includes a North-South component, as many countries in the Global South with already limited water resources produce water-intensive agricultural and other goods for export to countries in the Global North. This so-called "virtual water" may further contribute to water scarcity in the producing regions.

This chapter examines how mounting pressures on water resources can act as catalysts for conflict and argues that the current architecture of global water governance remains insufficiently equipped to address both present and future challenges. While water diplomacy – conceived as a comprehensive, multilevel diplomatic approach – offers significant potential to engage with the complex interlinkages between water and conflict, its effective implementation continues

2 See https://data.unicef.org/topic/water-and-sanitation/drinking-water/; 26.09.2025.

3 See https://dashboards.sdgindex.org/map/goals/sdg6/; 26.09.2025.

to face considerable obstacles. The chapter concludes by outlining key areas of action for the international community, with particular reference to the forthcoming United Nations Water Conference in 2026.

2. WATER AND CONFLICT

Water is mobile. It crosses borders and must be shared between two or more countries: 90% of the world's population has common resources with neighbouring countries, and there are 313 transboundary rivers and lakes around the world (UNECE/UNESCO/UN-Water 2024: 6). In addition, there are 468 known transboundary aquifers.[4] In total, 153 countries share at least one water basin with one or more other countries. Ismail Serageldin, then Vice-President of the World Bank, stated in 1995 that "the wars of the next century will be about water".[5] Today, 30 years later, there is broad consensus within the scientific community that water stress hardly ever leads directly to violent conflict (Michel 2020: 6). Most scholars emphasize that historically parties are more likely to value the merits of cooperation and decide to cooperate on scarce water resources than to start a conflict (Hussein et al. 2023: 1). Even if there are serious diplomatic tensions between two countries, they may still decide to cooperate on water resources. However, recent data suggests that the number of conflicts, both at the inter- and intrastate level, has been rising globally in recent years [see Figure 1]. 62% of the conflicts registered for 2023 were subnational, while only 38% involved two or more countries (Pacific Institute 2024: 2).

4 See https://un-igrac.org/latest/news/igrac-launches-new-transboundary-aquifers-of-the-world-map-2021/; 19.09.2025.

5 See http://www.serageldin.com/Organization/Details.aspx?id=4; 26.09.2025.

FIGURE 1: Water conflicts are on the rise

Water conflicts by type (2000–2023)

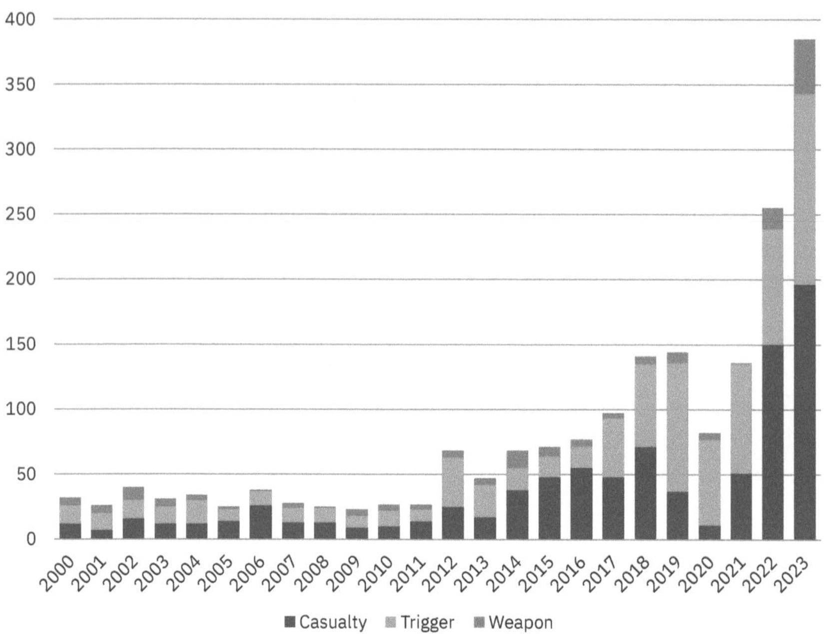

Legend:
Casualty: Water resources or water systems as casualty of conflict, where water resources, water systems, or people involved with the resource or the system, such as employees, are intentional or incidental casualties or targets of violence.
Trigger: Water as a trigger or root cause of conflict, where there is a dispute over the control of water or water systems or where economic or physical access to water, or scarcity of water, triggers violence.
Weapon: Water as a weapon of conflict, where water resources, or water systems themselves, are used as a tool or weapon in a violent conflict.

Source: Pacific Institute 2024: 2.

Noticeably, the distribution of water-related conflicts varies widely between different world regions [see Figure 2]. Central factors for the high prevalence of conflicts are clashes between farmers and pastoralists in Sub-Saharan Africa, increasing violence in the Middle East (Israel/Palestine, Yemen, Syria, Iraq) and in India (Pacific Institute 2024: 5–8, Gleick and Shimabuku 2023: 7–9), combined with high and increasing levels of water stress (Kuzma/Saccoccia/Chertrock 2023). The likelihood of water serving as a conflict driver is heightened in regions already affected by latent tensions, where such changes may operate as a "threat multiplier" (Koren/Bagozzi/Benson 2021: 68). Changes in water resources seldom translate directly into violent conflict; rather, their impact is mediated by societal capacities to address water-related challenges. Variations in water availability or access unfold within complex socio-environmental, technological, political, legal, and cultural contexts (Zareie/Bozorg-Haddad/Loáiciga 2021: 2338). Critical determinants include the dependence of key economic sectors – such as agriculture – on water, the degree of competition over scarce resources, and the technical capacity to augment supply.

FIGURE 2: Water conflicts are prevalent in Western and Southern Asia and Sub-Saharan Africa

Number of water conflicts by UN region (2000–2023)

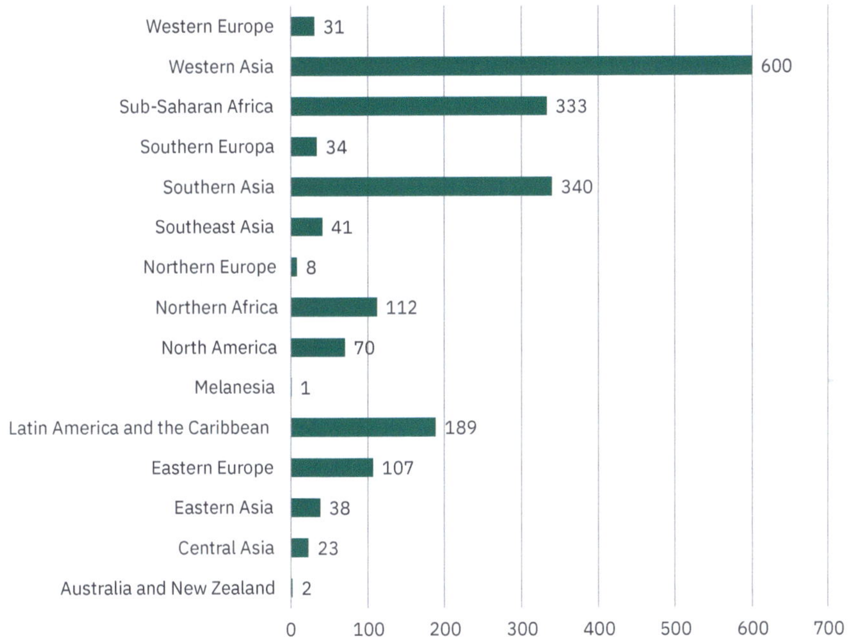

Source: Pacific Institute 2024: 3.

Water conflicts may arise from different pathways that mostly lead to changes in access to water or in the available quantity or quality of water. The availability of usable water may be triggered by environmental pressures such as reduced rainfall or saline intrusion, but also by changing demands from agriculture, urbanization or industry. Access to decision-making structures significantly shapes the degree of access to water resources. The occurrence of disasters such as floods, when coupled with limited resilience, can constitute additional conflict-triggering factors. Moreover, state-driven interventions may significantly affect water availability and access – for instance, through the construction of large-scale infrastructure projects such as dams or irrigation schemes that alter downstream water flows, or through the insufficient provision of adequate water and sanitation services (Michel 2020: 8–9). The functionality of state institutions and their ability to guarantee equitable access across all societal groups are central in shaping conflict dynamics (Michel 2020: 6, Krause et al. 2024: 1134). Unequal access to water exposes, reinforces, and amplifies existing power asymmetries (Krause et al. 2024: 1134, Zareie/Bozorg-Haddad/Loáiciga 2021: 2342). These pathways rarely operate in isolation; rather, it is the interplay of multiple factors that precipitates conflicts within a specific context.

Multiple water conflict pathways in southern Iraq

The situation in southern Iraq reveals the interconnectedness of several pathways, how stress on water resources may trigger conflicts in an already vulnerable region. Water flows from the Euphrates and Tigris rivers have decreased by 30% since the 1980s due to intensive use by agriculture and industry, the construction of dams (by Turkey, Iran, and Syria), damaged infrastructure, and climate change. At the same time, demand for water increases due to population growth, urbanization, and industrial uses. The latter combined with agricultural run-off and the discharge of untreated wastewater also impact on water quality, which cause waterborne diseases. As the government had neglected the maintenance of water infrastructure, only 73% of the population in urban areas and 40–45% in rural areas have access to safe water. Fragmented water governance within the country comes on top of this already challenging situation.

This situation led to conflicts between provincial authorities, between federal, provincial authorities and citizens, and between farmers, herders, and fishermen. Violent protests, partly fuelled by inadequate water supply and limited access, pose a threat to national security (Birkman/Kool/Struyken 2022).

The use of water either as a strategic means of increasing pressure on opposing parties or as a weapon, by both state and non-state actors is one conflict pathway, which has received increasing attention in recent years (Salameh 2024: 162, von Lossow/Houdret 2021: 29, Sers 2025: 992). This so-called "water weaponization" in armed conflicts has increased significantly since the early 21st century and has become particularly evident in recent conflicts in Gaza, Ukraine, and Syria

(Lopes/Gama 2025: 10, Sers 2025: 992). In Kurdish-controlled northeast Syria, which already suffered from years of severe droughts, Turkish authorities interrupted water supply and electricity for more than one million people, leading to the outbreak of diseases such as cholera (Sers 2025: 992). Deliberate attacks on water infrastructure by the Israeli government during the Israeli-Palestinian conflict have been intensively addressed by several UN organizations in recent years (Lopes/Gama 2025: 8–9). Water weaponization "can occur in multiple ways, namely by directly targeting water-related infrastructure, such as dams, dykes, and WASH facilities, and by contaminating water as a natural good through the use of poison or disease-causing agents" (Lopes/Gama 2025: 6). It has long-term effects on the environment and on health, e.g. through the spread of water-borne diseases or the destruction of health care infrastructure (Sers 2025: 992). Although the weaponization of water is a crime under international humanitarian law, it is increasingly accepted by countries as an appropriate means of warfare, either by themselves or by their allies (Sers 2025: 993). Lopes and Gama emphasize the mimicry effect, according to which the demonstrated efficacy of weaponizing water can function as a template for its replication in other contexts. Thus, "the increased practice of weaponizing water may contribute to further exacerbate ongoing violent effects" (Lopes/Gama 2025: 10).

Current global dynamics – marked by the resurgence of geopolitics and unilateralism, and the crisis of multilateralism – profoundly shape the management of scarce water resources among states sharing transboundary basins. Water is increasingly framed as an issue of national security rather than as a vital resource to which universal access must be ensured. The securitization of water may seriously compromise cooperation between countries competing for resources (Hussein et al. 2023: 2, Salameh 2024: 162), but it can also have significant negative impacts on distribution equity within a country (Gupta/Bosch/van Vliet 2025: 2). The construction of the Grand Ethiopian Renaissance Dam without adequate consultation of downstream countries may serve as a recent example for the securitization of water resources. Egypt has articulated the construction of the dam as a threat to its national water security. The Indus Water Treaty between India and Pakistan has survived severe political tensions and wars between the signatories. However, in response to a terrorist attack in Kashmir in April 2025, India temporarily suspended the treaty, employing it as a strategic instrument to exert pressure on Pakistan. This development reflects a broader trend: already in 2016,

India had reframed water from the Indus as a matter of national security (Singh/von Lossow 2025: 4).

Water securitization goes hand in hand with power asymmetries as a decisive factor for access to water resources (Fischhendler 2015: 250). When treating water first and foremost as a matter of national security, powerful states marginalize the relevance of water for livelihoods and development to the detriment of less powerful actors. Power is of relevance within countries and societies, but also at the international level, e.g. between upstream and downstream countries or between larger, economically more powerful countries and their smaller neighbours. The willingness to cooperate and mutually find viable solutions is declining, especially in already tense, conflictual situations.

Given the close interlinkages between water and conflict, the growing scarcity of water resources not only undermines livelihoods and hampers social and economic development but also poses risks to regional stability and may jeopardize peace and cooperation, particularly in fragile contexts; it thus turns into an issue of global concern (Herrfahrdt-Pähle et al. 2019: 3, Dombrowsky/Houdret/Ünver 2023). It is therefore in the interest of the international community to advance a more effective framework of global water governance capable of addressing the escalating challenges. Yet, current governance structures remain insufficiently equipped to fulfil this role.

3. THE FRAGMENTATION OF GLOBAL WATER GOVERNANCE

A coordinated and comprehensive water governance architecture can provide shared principles, norms, and institutions that help balance power asymmetries, enhance predictability, and build trust among riparian states (OECD 2015: 1–12, de Chazournes 2009: 1). They do not only provide the rules to which the signatory states commit themselves, but the principles enshrined in international frameworks also constitute an important reference point for negotiations between parties in transnational river basins (Schmeier 2021: 174–176, de Chazournes 2009: 1). According to the World Bank, it is still the case that "more than 2/3 of transboundary rivers lack any type of cooperative framework" (Deribe et al. 2024: 3), and only 43 out of 153 UN member states with transboundary waters have most of these water bodies covered by operational agreements (UNECE/UNESCO/UN-Water 2024: 21). In such cases, international law assumes a central role. A comprehensive and robust international legal framework is indispensable for fostering cooperation, preventing disputes, and ensuring the sustainable management of shared water resources in the face of escalating pressures (de Chazournes 2009: 10).

However, to date the global water governance structure is fragmented and not very coherent and effective (Herrfahrdt-Pähle et al. 2025: 5, Dombrowsky/Houdret/Ünver 2023, GCEW 2024: 191). Although a range of regimes and institutions addressing water operate at both global and regional levels [see Figure 3 for an overview], water governance continues to lack a robust global architecture comparable to that developed for issues such as climate change or biodiversity, notwithstanding its profound global significance. Most of the existing structures operate on a voluntary basis and thus depend on the political will of national governments or international institutions to cooperate. Two UN conventions provide international legal guidance, directly related to water: the "Convention on the Law of the Non-navigational Uses of International Watercourses" – UN Watercourses Convention (UNWC) – from 1997 and the "Convention on the Protection and Use of Transboundary Watercourses and International Lakes" – UNECE Water Convention – which was adopted in 1992, but only entered into force in 2016. Although both conventions constitute binding legal instruments that offer a valuable framework and normative orientation for addressing water-related conflicts, their enforcement mechanisms remain comparatively weak. The UNWC lacks an institutional body or secretariat; thus, implementation depends on the member states. Important actors, such as Ethiopia, Egypt, India, Pakistan, China, Turkey, and Brazil have not yet ratified the Convention. At the time of its entry into force, the convention was criticized as being already outdated, chiefly due to its limited consideration of environmental and human rights dimensions (Mager 2015: 14). The UNECE Water Convention only referred to Europe in the beginning, but it was opened to all UN member countries in 2016. Today, it is joined by 56 member states, still with a very strong focus on European countries[6] and thus a low global significance. In addition to these water-specific conventions, water figures with varying degrees of prominence in other UN conventions and governance frameworks.

6 See https://unece.org/member-states; 09.09.2025.

FIGURE 3: The international water regime remains fragmented and limited
Selected milestones in global water governance

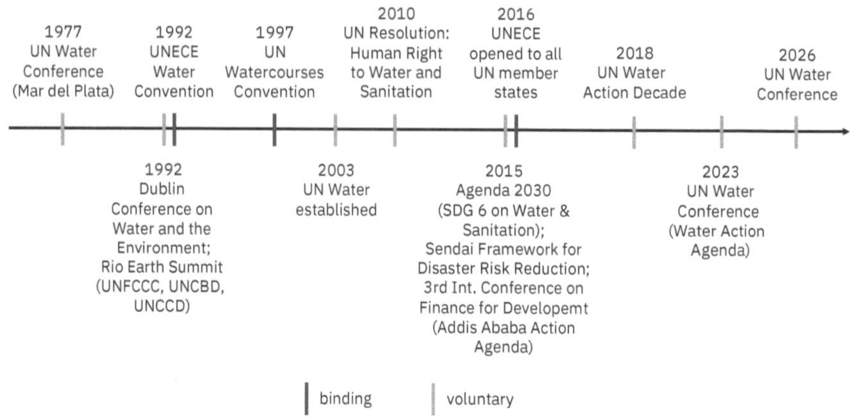

Note: UNECE = United Nations Economic Commission for Europe, UNFCCC = United Nations Framework Convention on Climate Change, UNCBD = United Nations Convention on Biological Diversity, UNCCD = United Nations Convention to Combat Desertification

Source: Own compilation.

Since 2003, UN-Water has served as the coordinating mechanism for the water-related activities of more than 30 UN entities. While not being a UN agency in its own right but rather a coordination platform, it is mandated to collect and disseminate information, data, and best practices on water issues and to provide toolkits to support national planning processes. UN-Water is also mandated to promote coherence within the UN system and to ensure that water is recognized as a cross-cutting issue in domains such as climate change, disaster risk reduction, gender, and human rights. Overall, UN-Water is important in terms of coordinating, facilitating, and raising awareness on water-related issues, but due to its limited mandate it largely depends on voluntary contributions from other UN agencies. Thus, its influence and impact on a fragmented and siloed global water governance remains rather low (GCEW 2024: 191).

The first United Nations Water Conference was held in Argentina in 1977. Forty-six years later, in 2023, approximately 10,000 participants convened in New York for its second session. Its major formal outcome was the Water Action Agenda – a compilation of over 700 commitments pledged by governments, nongovernmental stakeholders and private actors, covering finance, projects, policies, innovation, and cooperation.[7] However, only about 22% of the commitments made in the Water Action Agenda have quantitative targets, and often, clear financing options and timelines as well as monitoring mechanisms are missing. Despite the transboundary nature of water, only 12% of the commitments include cooperation across national borders or economic sectors (WRI 2023). Furthermore, all pledges are voluntary, which further limits accountability. The appointment of a UN Special Envoy on Water in 2024 to raise the visibility of water as a cross-cutting issue is a step in the right direction; however, it remains to be seen what she can achieve in such a complex siloed setting with multiple interests of a multitude of stakeholders. The upcoming UN Water Conference in December 2026 is expected, in light of the outcomes and critiques of the 2023 conference, to focus particularly on the implementation of the measures agreed in 2023 and on the mobilisation of corresponding funding. Particularly civil society organizations call for a strong focus on equity and inclusivity, which goes beyond symbolism. Strengthening global water governance and its coherence are other important issues to be discussed.

Parallel to these global developments, since the 1990s the growing pressure on global freshwater resources and the rise of water-related conflicts have strengthened the awareness that new approaches are needed at regional and national levels – approaches that move beyond the provision of technical solutions and explicitly recognize and address the complexity and diversity of conflict situations.

4. WATER DIPLOMACY IN TURBULENT TIMES

4.1 WATER DIPLOMACY AS A COMPREHENSIVE APPROACH TO ADDRESS COMPLEXITY

The concept of water diplomacy acknowledges that water management is "embedded in societal and political settings that go way beyond the water sector" (Sehring et al. 2022: 203) and that, consequently, policymakers and diplomats assume a critical function in this regard. Water diplomacy can be defined as

7 See https://sdgs.un.org/conferences/water2023/action-agenda and https://sdgs.un.org/partnerships/action-networks/water; 26.09.2025.

> "the deliberative political processes and practices of preventing, mitigating, and resolving disputes over transboundary water resources and developing joint water governance arrangements by applying foreign policy means, embedded in bi- and/or multilateral relations beyond the water sector and taking place at different tracks and levels" (Sehring et al. 2022: 212).

While alternative definitions of water diplomacy emphasize different dimensions, scholars largely concur on a set of core aspects, summarized by Keskinen, Salminen, and Haapala (2021: 3):

- Water diplomacy is a political process bringing together the different perspectives of stakeholders, also taking into account their senses of security, sovereignty, and national development priorities. Political processes must also consider the power relations between the various actors. While the broader political context exerts a significant influence on water diplomacy, the relationship is reciprocal, as water diplomacy can in turn facilitate regional interaction.
- As a preventive approach it focusses on conflict prevention and mediation, thus representing one of the normative foundations of water diplomacy. Regular exchange between parties and dispute-resolution mechanisms can reduce tensions and prevent that they turn into violent conflict.
- Through its integrative approach, water diplomacy goes beyond regional treaties and established mechanisms of transboundary cooperation among riparian governments, as it involves stakeholders from various levels and thematic sectors. This is also known as "multitrack diplomacy", bringing together science, policy, and practitioners. It supports legitimacy and the development of resilient solutions.
- Supporting cooperation is at the heart of water diplomacy processes. Identifying shared benefits and establishing trust between stakeholders are ultimate goals of this process. It rests on the stakeholders' willingness to engage in cooperation aimed at fostering the sustainable and equitable allocation of shared water resources.
- The technical dimension highlights the role of accurate and transparent data as a fundamental prerequisite for advancing water diplomacy. It further comprises the monitoring and evaluation of agreements concluded. Technical cooperation is diplomacy in practice and another important prerequisite for establishing trust.

The interplay of these five key aspects is contingent upon the specific context and the conflict-triggering factors inherent to the system under consideration.

4.2 WATER DIPLOMACY IN PRACTICE

Water diplomacy relies on a repertoire of context-specific tools and instruments on multiple levels, tailored to distinct forms of water stress and related conflicts, while accounting for the power relations, perspectives, and expectations of the actors involved. They can be grouped into four categories [see Table 1].

TABLE 1: Water diplomacy follows different logics and perspectives
Tools and instruments of water diplomacy

Category	Examples
Formal diplomatic	• multilateral treaties (UNECE, UN Watercourses Convention) • regional treaties and agreements (e. g. Mekong Agreement, Indus Water Treaty) • joint institutions (river basin organizations, e. g. Nile Basin Initiative, Mekong River Commission)
Diplomatic & mediation	• third-party mediation (international organizations, regional organizations, UN, other countries) • track II diplomacy (informal dialogues, academic or NGO-led initiatives) • trust-building activities (regular exchanges, notification of planned measures)
Technical & scientific	• data-sharing portals (Mekong hydrological database, Danube monitoring programme) • modeling and monitoring frameworks • scientific networks
Cooperative & benefit-sharing	• joint infrastructure (e. g. dams, hydropower plants) • multilevel governance platforms • capacity-building programmes

The first category encompasses "hard" legal and normative instruments, including binding treaties and joint institutions mandated with their implementation. Such legal frameworks are pivotal in fostering legitimacy, predictability, and accountability, thereby constituting a foundational basis for conflict prevention. Diplomatic and mediation instruments illustrate the integrative nature of water diplomacy, as they engage both third parties and a broad range of national stakeholders. They lay the ground for establishing trust between the different parties and for integrating questions of equity and meaningful participation into the discussion. Next, technical activities provide an evidence base for informed decisions, they increase transparency, and through joint programmes they can also strengthen the sense of cooperation. Finally, tools for identifying mutual gains are to provide (economic) incentives for long-term cooperation. In practice, water diplomacy processes combine various tools and instruments.

Tools and instruments in water diplomacy processes

Mekong Agreement and Mekong River Commission (MRC)

The Mekong Agreement created the MRC, an institutional platform that applies multiple tools: joint monitoring networks, data portals, scenario modelling, and prior consultation procedures for major projects. Technical studies on dams, sediment transport, and fisheries illustrate how science-based analysis informs diplomacy. The MRC's dialogue forums and basin development planning mechanisms serve as instruments that prevent disputes from escalating, balancing development needs with environmental and social safeguards across the basin. A distinctive instrument is the Procedures for Notification, Prior Consultation and Agreement, which require states to inform and consult one another before undertaking significant projects such as mainstream dams. At the downside, the MRC lacks binding dispute resolution powers, and key upstream states – China and Myanmar – are not full members, limiting its authority.

Nile Basin Initiative (NBI)

The NBI is a transitional cooperative framework, focussing on trust-building and technical cooperation among the basin's ten riparian states. Its tools include joint modelling and scenario analysis, the Subsidiary Action Programs (ENTRO and NELSAP) for sub-basin projects, and cooperative planning frameworks funded by international partners. By promoting benefit-sharing investments in irrigation, hydropower, and watershed management, the NBI shifted focus from allocation disputes to shared development. Its reliance on voluntary compliance and dialogue implies that it lacks strong enforcement or dispute resolution powers. Lack of technical, personal, and technical resources are further challenges. Serious tensions remain over the construction of the Grand Ethiopian Renaissance Dam.

Third parties – such as non-riparian states, intergovernmental organizations, or development agencies – play an important role in supporting disputing actors in the identification of joint solutions and the promotion of benefit-sharing (Michel 2020: 25; Salameh 2024: 166). They contribute to embedding negotiations within international standards and principles, thereby strengthening compliance and legitimacy. By assuming mediating functions, they can facilitate trust-building among stakeholders, which constitutes a critical precondition for the willingness to compromise and reach agreement (Keskinen/Salminen/Haapala 2021: 2). In addition, third parties may provide technical expertise or financial resources, helping to generate reliable and unbiased data as a foundation for evidence-based negotiations (Sehring et al. 2022: 217). Beyond mediation, third parties may further contribute to long-term capacity building, institutional development, and the alignment of basin-level processes with broader global agendas such as climate adaptation and the SDGs. Their involvement can also mitigate power asymmetries between riparian states and ensure that weaker actors retain a voice in decision-making processes. The Middle East Council on Global Affairs, e. g., explicitly calls for a stronger multilateral engagement in the region of the Middle East and North Africa (MENA) to prevent further escalation regarding the management of water resources (Hawash/Ghafar 2025: 7). However, there is reason to fear that the currently growing scepticism towards international cooperation may also weaken the potential role of international actors, organizations or states to act as mediators in deadlocked conflicts.

The effectiveness of regional institutions is another key factor for successful water diplomacy processes. Several river basin organizations (RBOs) have been established in order to implement regional agreements and lead the processes for the sustainable and equitable management of transboundary water resources. There are more than 120 RBOs around the world (Deribe et al. 2024: 3), the International Commissions for the Protection of the Danube River and the Rhine, the Mekong River Commission, and the Nile Basin Initiative being prominent examples. The main task of RBOs is to foster cooperation and exchange of information and data between the riparian states and external partners. They establish rules of engagement, build capacities among national agencies, enforce and monitor the implementation of agreements, and manage emerging conflicts (Dombrowsky/Hensengerth 2018: 4). RBOs thus play a pivotal role in advancing effective transboundary water management (Deribe et al. 2024: 3). However, their effectiveness is highly contingent upon their institutional and operational capacities (Hussein et al. 2023: 5, Deribe et al. 2024: 14). Empirical studies demonstrate that RBOs often struggle to fully realize their mandates due to deficiencies in technical expertise for data provision, limited legal authority and lack of enforcement mechanisms, as well as shortages of skilled personnel and sustainable funding (Hawash/Ghafar 2025: 5, Prniyazova et al. 2025: 13). Moreover, political tensions and mutual mistrust among riparian actors may further constrain their performance and overall effectiveness (Salameh 2024: 166, Deribe et al. 2024: 12).

5. THE INTERPLAY BETWEEN WATER DIPLOMACY AND GLOBAL WATER GOVERNANCE

The analysis highlights that water diplomacy holds considerable potential to mediate the intricate nexus between freshwater resources and conflict dynamics. Yet, the discernible rise in water-related disputes illustrates how intensifying pressures on freshwater systems, coupled with the current surge in protectionism and the erosion of multilateralism, are increasingly testing the limits of diplomatic engagement. While water diplomacy is typically associated with activities at the regional and subnational levels, the establishment of a robust global water governance architecture, anchored in binding norms and principles, may provide an essential guiding framework for diplomatic processes and enhance accountability in water-related negotiations. In this regard, global water governance and international water law constitute integral and indispensable dimensions of water diplomacy (Schmeier 2021: 174). Conversely, successful water diplomacy processes may feed back into the global water governance regime, thereby also contributing to greater coherence and effectiveness on the global level. A combined approach addressing water-related conflicts across global, national, and local scales can mediate divergent interests and, through clear regulatory frameworks and joint solutions, help mitigate unequal power relations among stakeholders.

6. THE WAY FORWARD

The resumption of the UN Water Conferences with the next conference scheduled for December 2026 provides a strong momentum to strengthen water diplomacy, i.e. through the following means:

- **Do not leave water problems only to water departments:**
  Complexity must be embraced, when dealing with challenges regarding the distribution of scarce water resources, particularly in conflict-prone settings. Although water management entails technical dimensions requiring special-

ized expertise, it is fundamentally conditioned by political and social factors. Achieving sustainable solutions therefore necessitates comprehensive political responses that integrate social, cultural, environmental, and economic considerations. There are no easy fixes for complex problems.

- **Strengthen coherence of global water governance:**
  The upcoming UN Water Conference in 2026 should seek to strengthen coherence and accountability in global water governance, thereby reinforcing the effectiveness of the existing governance architecture and addressing prevailing trends of declining cooperation and the securitization of water resources at the national level. Due to the cross-cutting nature of water and the increasing urgency of the water challenge, silo thinking must be ended and coherence with other global processes must be strengthened. Considering the severe impacts of climate change on global water resources, this call for coherence refers particularly to the UN Framework Convention on Climate Change and the Paris Agreement. The international community must support the Special Envoy in her challenging task of strengthening overall global coordination on water issues.

- **Third-party engagement can make a difference:**
  Due to the global implications of the water crisis, it should be in the interest of the international community to support processes aimed at improving cooperation, especially in conflict-prone settings. Such support is particularly important considering the key role of often underequipped river basin organizations.

REFERENCES

Birkman, Laura/Kool, Dorith/Struyken, Eva 2022: Water Challenges and Conflict Dynamics in Southern Iraq. An In-Depth Analysis of an Under-Researched Crisis, Report Water, Peace and Security, Delft.

De Chazournes, Laurence Boisson 2009: Freshwater and International Law. The Interplay between Universal, Regional and Basin Perspectives (The United Nations World Water Assessment Programme Insights), Paris.

Deribe, Mekdalewit M./Melesse, Assefa M./Kidanewold, Belete B./Dinar, Shlomi/ Anderson, Elizabeth P. 2024: Assessing International Transboundary Water Management Practices to Extract Contextual Lessons for the Nile River Basin, in: Water 16: 14, 1960. Dombrowsky, Ines/Hensengerth, Oliver 2018: Governing the Water-Energy-Food Nexus Related to Hydropower on Shared Rivers: The Role of Regional Organizations, in: Frontiers in Environmental Science 6: 153.

Dombrowsky, Ines/Houdret, Annabelle/Ünver, Olcay 2023: The UN Water Conference. Time to Govern Water as a Global Commons (The Current Column, German Institute of Development and Sustainability) Bonn.

Fischhendler, Itay 2015: The Securitization of Water Discourse. Theoretical Foundations, Research Gaps and Objectives of the Special Issue, in: International Environmental Agreements 15, 245–255.

Gleick, Peter H./Shimabuku, Morgan 2023: Water-Related Conflicts. Definitions, Data, and Trends From the Water Conflict Chronology, in: Environmental Research Letters 18: 3, 034022.

Global Commission on the Economics of Water 2024 (GCEW): The Economics of Water. Valuing the Hydrological Cycle as a Global Common Good, Paris.

Gupta, Joyeeta/Bosch, Hilmer J./van Vliet, Luc 2025: Water Security Reframed Using Water System Justice and Earth System Boundaries, Foundations, and Corridor, in: Frontiers in Water 7, 1520853.

Hawash, Mohammad Abu/Ghafar, Adel Abdel 2025: Water Diplomacy. How to Prevent Water Wars in the MENA Region (Issue Brief, Middle East Council on Global Affairs), Doha.

Herrfahrdt-Pähle, Elke/Houdret, Annabelle/Dombrowsky, Ines/Cullmann, Johannes/Mukherji, Aditi/Unver, Olcay/Varady, Robert 2025: Empowering Global Water Governance. Taking the 2023 UN Water Conference Outcomes Forward to Address the Current Water Crises, in: Water International 50: 1, 4–10.

Herrfahrdt-Pähle, Elke/Scheumann, Waltina/Houdret, Annabelle/Dombrowsky, Ines 2019: Freshwater as a Global Commons. International Governance and the Role of Germany (Discussion Paper 15/2019, German Development Institute/Deutsches Institut für Entwicklungspolitik), Bonn.

Hussein, Hussam/Campbell, Zoe/Leather, Josephine/Ryce, Patrick 2023: Putting Diplomacy at the Forefront of Water Diplomacy, in: PLOS Water 2: 9, e0000173.

Keskinen, Marko/Salminen, Erik/Haapala, Juho 2021: Water Diplomacy Paths. An Approach to Recognise Water Diplomacy Actions in Shared Waters, in: Journal of Hydrology 602, 126737.

Koren, Ore/Bagozzi, Benjamin E./Benson, Thomas S. 2021: Food and Water Insecurity as Causes of Social Unrest. Evidence from Geolocated Twitter Data, in: Journal of Peace Research 58: 1, 67–82.

Krause, Stefan/Lynch, Iseult/Agarwal, Ankit/Akinsemolu, Adenike/Arheimer, Berit/Buytaert, Wouter/Floyd, Rita/Houdret, Annabelle/Saccoccia, Elizabeth/Schneidewind, Uwe/Tockner, Klement/Yasmin, Tahmina/Hannah, David M. 2024: Seven Strategies to Leverage Water for Peace and Foster Sustainable and Just Water Management for All, in: Nature Water 2: 12, 1134–1138.

Kuzma, Samantha/Saccoccia, Liz/Chertrock, Marlena 2023: 25 Countries, Housing One-Quarter of the Population, Face Extremely High Water Stress, Washington, DC (https://www.wri.org/insights/highest-water-stressed-countries, 29.09.2025).

Lopes, Paula Duarte/Gama, Margarida 2025: Reviewing Water Wars and Water Weaponisation Literatures. Is there an Unnoticed Link?, in: Water 17: 6, 897.

Mager, Ute 2015: International Water Law. Global Developments and Regional Examples, Heidelberg.

Michel, David 2020: Water Conflict Pathways and Peacebuilding Strategies (Peaceworks, No. 164) Washington, DC.

Organisation for Economic Co-operation and Development (OECD) 2015: Stakeholder Engagement for Inclusive Water Governance, Paris.

Pacific Institute 2024: Fact Sheet. Water Conflict Chronology Update, Oakland (https://pacinst.org/wp-content/uploads/2024/08/Water-Conflict-Chronology_Fact-Sheet.pdf, 29.09.2025).

Prniyazova, Albina/Turaeva, Suriya/Turgunov, Daniyar/Jarihani, Ben 2025: Sustainable Transboundary Water Governance in Central Asia. Challenges, Conflicts, and Regional Cooperation, in: Sustainability 17: 11, 4968.

Salameh, Mohammed Torki Bani 2024: Challenges and Opportunities in Water Diplomacy. A Middle Eastern Perspective, in: Jeon, Han-Yong (ed.): Sustainable Development of Water and Environment (Proceedings of ICSDWE 2024), Cham, 161–171.

Schmeier, Susanne 2021: International Water Law Principles in Negotiations and Water Diplomacy, in: American Journal of International Law – AJIL Unbound 115, 173–177.

Sehring, Jenniver/Schmeier, Susanne/Horst, Rozemarijn ter/Offutt, Alyssa/Sharipova, Bota 2022: Diving into Water Diplomacy. Exploring the Emergence of a Concept, in: Diplomatica 4: 2, 200–221.

Sers, Rebecca 2025: The Weaponisation of Water, in: The Lancet 406: 10507, 992–994.

Singh, Akanksha/von Lossow, Tobias 2025: Indus Water Treaty 2025 – A Pause of Cooperation, not an End (Clingendael Alert), Wassenaar.

United Nations Economic Commission for Europe (UNECE)/United Nations Educational, Scientific and Cultural Organization (UNESCO)/UN-Water (2024): Progress on Transboundary Water Cooperation. Mid-term Status of SDG Indicator 6.5.2 with a Special Focus on Climate Change, Paris.

von Lossow, Tobias/Houdret, Annabelle 2021: Wasser auf die Mühlen der Entwicklungsziele, in: Aus Politik und Zeitgeschichte 12/2021, 25–32 (https://www.bpb.de/shop/zeitschriften/apuz/wasser-2021/328627/wasser-auf-die-muehlen-der-entwicklungsziele/, 18.09.2025).

World Resources Institute (WRI) 2023: UN Water Conference 2023: Not Enough Game-Changing Commitments. Commentary, Washington, DC (https://www.wri.org/insights/un-water-conference-2023-needed-outcomes, 18.09.2025).

Zareie, Soheila/Bozorg-Haddad, Omid/Loáiciga, Hugo A. 2021: A State-of-the-Art Review of Water Diplomacy, in: Environment, Development and Sustainability 23: 2, 2337–2357.

LIST OF CONTRIBUTORS

Markus Ciesielski

is Professor of Political Sciences and Social Policy at the University of Applied Sciences Saarbrücken and Senior Associate Fellow at the Institute for Development and Peace (INEF) at the University of Duisburg-Essen. He holds a doctorate in social sciences, and his research focuses on social inequality, legal mobilization and legal transformation, access to justice, sociology of law and governance.

Christof Hartmann

is Professor of Political Science, International Relations and African Politics, at the Institute of Political Science and Director of the Institute for Development and Peace (INEF) at the University of Duisburg-Essen. He holds a Ph.D in political science, and his research focuses on the dynamics of change in political institutions in African countries, regionalism in the Global South (especially Africa), Africa's foreign relations (especially with China), development policy as well as the role of political institutions for conflict prevention and mitigation.

Marcus Kaplan

is the Executive Director of the Foundation for Development and Peace (sef:) in Bonn. He holds a doctorate in geography and works on issues of global sustainability and the implementation of the UN Sustainable Development Goals (SDGs), the links between sustainable development and peacebuilding, and the evaluation of international development cooperation.

Christian Scheper

is Senior Researcher at the Institute for Development and Peace (INEF) at the University of Duisburg-Essen. He holds a doctorate in political science. A key focus of his work is the regulation of global supply chains and production networks. He also conducts research on human rights, labour rights and sustainability in the global economy, as well as global governance and transnational corporations.

Cornelia Ulbert

is the Executive Director of the Institute for Development and Peace (INEF) at the University of Duisburg-Essen. She holds a doctorate in political science, and her work focuses on issues such as global governance, the implementation of the UN Sustainable Development Goals (SDGs) and, in particular, the role of partnerships and non-state actors (civil society, private foundations) with a focus on global health.

INDEX